Save Smart *for a* Secure Future

Save Smart *for a* Secure Future

The essential guide to achieving your retirement dreams

WILLIAM T. SPITZ

Macmillan • USA

MACMILLAN
A Simon & Schuster Macmillan Company
1633 Broadway
New York, NY 10019-6785

Macmillan Publishing books may be purchased for business or sales promotional use. For information please write: Special Markets Department, Macmillan Publishing USA, 1633 Broadway, New York, NY 10019.

Copyright © 1998 by William T. Spitz

All rights reserved. No part of this book may be reproduced or transmitted in any form or by any means, electronic or mechanical, including photocopying, recording, or by any information storage or retrieval system, without permission in writing from the Publisher.

MACMILLAN is a trademark of Macmillan, Inc.

Library of Congress Cataloging-in-Publication Data

Spitz, William T.
Save smart for a secure future: the essential guide to achieving your retirement dreams / William T. Spitz.
p. cm.
Includes index.
ISBN 0-02-861841-6
1. Finance, Personal. 2. Investments. 3. Portfolio management.
I. Title.
HG179.S5555   1998
332.024—dc21   97-15841
CIP

Printed in the United States of America
10 9 8 7 6 5 4 3 2 1

Book design by Kevin Hanek

The author and publisher specifically disclaim any responsibility for liability, loss, or risk, personal or otherwise, which is incurred as a consequence, directly or indirectly, of the use and application of any of the contents in this book.

ADVANCE PRAISE FOR *SAVE SMART FOR A SECURE FUTURE*

"Planning for retirement is a critically important issue for everyone. William Spitz's readable and down-to-earth book helps demystify the subject. It can help anyone get started on the road toward saving and investing for a secure and rewarding retirement."
—Daniel P. Tully, Chairman Emeritus, Merrill Lynch & Co., Inc.

"For an introductory or secondary tutorial on retirement planning, you can't do better than Bill Spitz's new book. It runs the gamut on beginning, developing, and sticking with a retirement program. I'd recommend it for anyone."
—Kenneth L. Fisher, Chairman, Fisher Investments, Inc. and *Forbes* magazine "Portfolio Strategy" columnist

"Bill Spitz will tuck you and your retirement plan into bed easier than any financial planning book I've read. Clear, concise, and thoroughly readable, it could be your first giant step toward understanding the complicated world of asset allocation and making it pay-off in the years ahead."
—William H. Gross, Managing Director, Pacific Investment Management Company

Contents

CHAPTER 1 • This Is Your Life 1

CHAPTER 2 • The ABCs of Retirement Plans 11

CHAPTER 3 • How Much Should You Contribute to Your Retirement Plan? 33

CHAPTER 4 • A Primer on Investments 47

CHAPTER 5 • Investment Risk 71

CHAPTER 6 • Creating a Portfolio 105

CHAPTER 7 • Selecting Mutual Funds and Insurance Products 135

CHAPTER 8 • Step Up to the Plate 163

Glossary 171

Index 179

CHAPTER 1

This Is Your Life

Opportunity is what happens when luck and preparation meet.

—Oprah Winfrey

Once in a while, each of us lapses into a daydream about the simple and carefree life that existed during the "good old days." In fact, life was never really all that simple, but the passage of time has a way of cloaking our memories in a soft and pleasant glow. While most things do not change very much with time, one facet of life that *has* become more complicated is the challenge of saving for retirement.

In all likelihood, your father spent the majority of his career with one employer and was rewarded with a pension that provided a comfortable and predictable standard of living during retirement. During his career, he didn't have to worry about how much to save or where to invest his funds because all of those problems were handled by the company. After retirement, his pension check was supplemented by Social Security, which was viewed as a pillar of financial strength and stability. He could also count on Medicare to provide at least a moderate level of health care.

What a difference a generation makes! Today, the press is filled with articles on the shaky finances of both Social Security and the Medicare system, and public opinion polls indicate that most baby boomers do not expect to receive either benefit when they reach retirement age. Equally important, many employers have replaced traditional pensions with 401(k) and other similar retirement plans that require the employee to make a number of critical decisions.

For example, an employee must first decide how much to contribute to her retirement fund. Next, she is asked to select from among a number of investment options including mutual funds, insurance products, and the company's own stock. While the company generally tries to be helpful by providing information on various investments, most people understandably find this decision both unfamiliar and threatening. Finally, when the employee reaches retirement age, she is faced with a great deal of flexibility as to how she receives her retirement benefit. Which of the many payment options should she choose?

Most important, all of these decisions affect the amount of income the employee will receive during retirement. In other words, the employee is at risk since the company does not guarantee a fixed monthly benefit. Instead, her retirement income is determined by the size of the fund that she accumulates during her career. In simple terms, Corporate America has shifted a good bit of the responsibility for retirement security to its employees.

THE OPPORTUNITY OF A LIFETIME

If you work for an employer that offers a 401(k), 403(b), 457, or similar plan, you will be forced to make these critical investment decisions. While taking control of your retirement program could be considered a heavy responsibility, you will be better served by viewing it as a great opportunity. This book is designed to help you make the most of that opportunity.

What's so great about assuming responsibility for your investments? First, the investment world is fascinating, since it touches economics, politics, world affairs, technology, and just about every other aspect of life. Additionally, investing is fun. Most important, if you devote enough of your time to doing a first-class job of managing your retirement program, you will be the beneficiary! And finally, the potential impact of doing a good job is tremendous.

To illustrate this point, consider two twenty-five-year-old friends who are each contributing 10% of salary to a retirement plan. The first individual earns an annual return during his forty-year career of 8%. With just a little bit of extra knowledge and good planning, the second manages a 9% return. At retirement, the second individual will have accumulated 25% more money than his friend, which will translate directly into a 25% increase in retirement income. And this tremendous improvement in lifestyle resulted from a mere 1% increase in return. Think about the potential impact of a 2% or 3% increase in return!

This simple example demonstrates the power of a very important concept known as compound interest. At the end of one year, a $100 investment that earns a 10% return will be valued at $110. Assuming the $10 in earnings is reinvested rather than spent, the second year's earnings will be 10% of $110, or $11. In year three, the investment will earn $12.10, and so on.

Compound interest is a powerful force, because investment earnings increase every year, and at an accelerating rate. This basic financial principle has two important implications for retirement savers. First, it is not necessary to earn large returns in order to accumulate a substantial retirement fund. By consistently earning a reasonable rate of return, most diligent savers should be able to accomplish their retirement objectives. Second, as was demonstrated above, small increases in return have a large cumulative impact on wealth.

The approach to saving for retirement that is outlined in this book is based on these two principles. First, you will learn to design an investment program that should deliver consistent returns in most environments. Moreover, because every investment entails risk of one kind or another, we will structure your investments to make sure that you understand and are comfortable with the amount of risk that you assume. Finally, by carefully selecting the investments that you include in your retirement plan, you should be able to squeeze out a little extra return. Of course, there are no guarantees or sure things in the investment world. But this book should provide you with the knowledge and self-confidence to do a first-class job of managing your retirement assets.

THE KEY TO SUCCESS

The world of finance seems both mysterious and complex, and many people are intimidated to the point that they do not believe that they can be successful investors. The truth is quite the contrary. You can successfully prepare for retirement by following three simple but important rules:

> Rule 1. Begin saving as early as possible, and save consistently throughout your career.
>
> Rule 2. Develop a well-organized investment program that is specifically tailored to your needs.
>
> Rule 3. Stick with your program. Don't allow the normal ups and downs of the markets to interfere with your long-range objectives.

Let's examine each of these in more detail.

Rule 1—Save Consistently

Chapter 3 provides a good deal of information to help you determine how much you should be contributing to your retirement fund every year. Without burdening you with all of the details just yet, an individual who begins saving at age twenty-five should put aside about 10% of salary to ensure a comfortable standard of living during retirement. While a savings rate of 10% may seem unattainable, remember that most employers match an employee's contribution to some extent.

Now, let's assume that the employee does not begin to save until age thirty-five. At that point, she will be forced to save 17.9% of salary for the rest of her career. In total, she will contribute 50% more dollars in order to end up in the same place. Even with a healthy matching contribution by the company, very few people are able to save at this level. The moral of the story is that the power of compound interest makes it much easier to succeed if you start early.

Rule 2—Get Organized

This book is based on the belief that success results from approaching retirement planning in an organized, businesslike manner. In other words, you need to develop and implement an investment program. At this point, let's briefly preview the five steps that you will follow to meet your retirement goals:

Five Steps to an Investment Program

Step 1. Establish your investment objectives.

Step 2. Decide which types of investments to include in your retirement portfolio.

Step 3. Divide your savings among these categories in the optimal proportions.

Step 4. Select mutual funds in each category.

Step 5. Review and update your program at least once every year.

The first step is to determine the standard of living that you expect during retirement. This decision will dictate the amount you should save, the return you need to earn on your investments, and the level of risk you will assume. While everyone would like to minimize risk, a lower level of risk almost always implies a lower rate of return. Therefore, you should choose a conservative approach to investing only after carefully evaluating the true nature of investment risk, as well as your personal circumstances.

Once you know where you are headed with your program, the next step is to choose the types of securities in which to invest. Chapter 4 provides a good deal of information on the various options that are commonly available through 401(k) plans.

Next, you will select a blend of these various types of investments in order to achieve the best balance between risk and return.

These first three steps represent the framework of your program. Step four, then, is to actually select mutual funds or insurance products from among those offered by your plan. Chapter 7 emphasizes the importance of evaluating many criteria rather than simply selecting the fund with the best return over the previous few years.

Finally, once every year or so, you need to review your program to make sure that everything is on track, and to make any mid-course corrections that are required.

Why is an organized approach to retirement planning so important? First, each individual's needs are different. Different investments, therefore, are right for different individuals. How will you know which is appropriate for you unless you first establish some objectives and guidelines? Second, controlling risk is a key ingredient of success. It really isn't that difficult, but you must include the right kinds of investments in your retirement plan and in the correct proportions. Third, you need to know if your goals are not being met in order to adjust your strategy. While all of these are important, the most persuasive reason for taking an organized approach is related to Rule 3.

RULE 3—STICK WITH THE PROGRAM

Human beings are emotional animals who are easily influenced by the herd mentality. When Wall Street is surging ahead and the financial press is full of rosy predictions, it is easy and comfortable to jump on board. Similarly, gloom and uncertainty make it awfully tempting to sell at the bottom of a market downturn.

Most of the time, these emotional decisions are wrong, and they can be financially disastrous. By establishing and sticking with an organized investment program, you will have the knowledge and confidence to ride out the ups and downs without overreacting.

THIS IS YOUR LIFE

We are now ready to dive into the nitty-gritty. Planning for retirement is not that difficult, and a modest commitment of time and energy on your part can have a meaningful impact on your future. After all, it's your money and your life!

Because each retirement plan is unique, you will need to contact the Human Resources department at your employer to get specific details on your plan and the investment options available to you. However, this book provides everything you need to know about saving and investing. Only three things are not included: patience, discipline, and commitment. They are your responsibility.

Key Points to Remember

- Save regularly.
- Get organized.
- Stick with the plan.

CHAPTER 2

The ABCs of Retirement Plans

Education will never become as expensive as ignorance.

—JESSE JACKSON

The Human Resources department of your employer faces an uphill battle in coping with the volumes of constantly changing regulations from the Internal Revenue Service and Department of Labor that govern retirement plans. Luckily, as a participant, you need only concentrate on a couple of critical areas. In particular, you need to know:

- How much money you can contribute to your plan every year.
- What happens if you need to withdraw money from your retirement plan.

- What happens to your retirement plan if you change employers.

- Whether you can move your money from one investment option to another.

- What options will be available to you at retirement, and when must you begin to receive distributions from your accumulated funds.

This chapter will deal with each of these issues. However, the scope of this book allows for only a brief review of these topics. Moreover, government regulations vary according to the type of plan and employers have the right to impose additional restrictions. Therefore, please consult the Human Resources department of your employer and your tax adviser for more details.

Before getting into the specifics, a broad overview of retirement plans might be helpful.

DEFINED BENEFIT VERSUS DEFINED CONTRIBUTION PLANS

Defined benefit and **defined contribution** represent the two basic types of retirement plans. A defined benefit, or DB, plan is the traditional, carefree pension that your father probably enjoyed. In a DB plan, an employee's retirement benefit is calculated according to a formula that normally takes into account his salary history and the number of years that he has worked for the company. This benefit is guaranteed and must be paid whether or not the company has accumulated enough assets in the pension plan to meet the payment requirement. In other words, the company assumes all of the risk. In addition, the government imposes complex accounting and reporting responsibilities on companies with DB plans. From the standpoint of the employee, there is also a serious negative in that he will not receive any benefit if he leaves the company prior to a certain date, which is called the "vesting" date.

Not surprisingly, all of these negatives have induced many employers to abandon DB plans for defined contribution (DC) plans, which include 401(k), 403(b), 457, and SEP plans. While the details of each type of plan vary, the basic structure is the same. In a defined contribution plan, the amounts of the employee's contribution as well as any match from his employer are defined by IRS regulations and the documents governing the plan. As was mentioned in Chapter 1, the employee is generally responsible for choosing among the investment options that his employer makes available, and his income during retirement is a function of both the amount he saves and his success as an investor. Therefore, the employee bears a portion of the cost of the plan, since he is asked to make contributions from his salary and also assumes all of the investment risk. In addition, the employer is relieved of a great deal of the reporting responsibility.

While DC plans may seem one-sided, there are benefits to the employee as well. First, he may be able to save enough to achieve a better standard of living during retirement than a DB plan would have provided. Second, a participant in a defined contribution plan generally has more flexibility as to how he withdraws his accumulated funds during retirement. Most important, defined contribution plans are usually portable, which means that the employee can take his fund with him if he changes jobs. However, while the employee's own contributions are fully portable, he may forfeit some of the employer's matching contributions if he leaves the company prior to the vesting date.

The defined contribution plan that applies to you depends upon the nature of your employer. While you may actually be able to use several of these plans, the basic lineup is as follows:

TYPE OF PLAN	TYPE OF EMPLOYER
401(k)	For-profit company
403(b)	Not-for-profit entity (charitable organizations, educational institutions, etc.)
457	State and local government
SEP	Self-employed and small companies

Self-employed individuals can choose among three different alternatives known as SEP-IRA, Keogh, and SAR-SEP plans. They differ as to the amount an employee can contribute, as well as his ability to vary the contribution from year to year. Moreover, these alternatives have significantly different administrative and reporting requirements. Recent legislation provides small businesses with a new type of plan called "simple," which can be structured as a 401(k) plan or as separate IRAs for each employee. You may want to contact your advisers in order to compare this new option with other alternatives. For the purposes of this book, the discussion of SEP plans will be limited to the SEP-IRA, which offers the most simplicity and ease of administration.

Let's now turn to the key areas of concern that were listed above.

HOW MUCH CAN YOU CONTRIBUTE TO YOUR PLAN?

First, you should understand that each retirement plan is governed by rules established by the employer within the broader framework of government regulations. Therefore, your employer is free to establish minimum and maximum contribution levels that may differ from the IRS limits. The following bullets summarize the maximum contribution guidelines for each type of plan under current government regulations:

- **401(k) Plans** Employee contribution: 20% of salary, subject to an annual maximum of $9,500. Total contribution including employer match is limited to the lesser of 25% of W-2 compensation or $30,000.

- **403(b) Plans** Employee contribution: 20% of salary, subject to an annual maximum of $9,500. The regulations include a "catch-up" provision that allows an employee to temporarily increase contributions to make up for years in which he did not participate in the plan. Total contribution including any employer match is limited to $30,000 per year.

- **457 Plans** 25% of salary, subject to an annual maximum of $7,500. A "catch-up" provision applies to individuals approaching retirement age.

- **SEP-IRA** 15% of self-employment earnings, subject to an annual maximum of $22,500.

In the case of 401(k) and 403(b) plans, the $9,500 maximum employee contribution is increased annually by the rate of inflation. Some individuals may be able to participate in several different plans, but their total contribution to all retirement plans is limited to $30,000.

The maximum contribution rules are generally of more concern to individuals with very high incomes, because very few people have the ability to save at the permitted level of 15% to 25% of salary. A larger number of people will be affected by a minimum standard imposed by an employer, such as a requirement that an employee contribute at least 5% of salary in order to participate in the plan. A savings rate of 5% may be a difficult first step for someone who has not been saving due to a tight budget. In addition to budget constraints, many people choose not to participate in retirement plans because they want to be able to gain access to their funds in case of an emergency. Therefore, it is important to understand the circumstances under which money can be withdrawn from a retirement plan.

WHAT HAPPENS IF YOU NEED TO TAKE MONEY OUT OF YOUR RETIREMENT FUND?

As you will see in a moment, many plans impose restrictions on removing funds, and any withdrawal may result in unfavorable tax consequences. Besides, any funds that you remove will reduce your standard of living during retirement or force you to make substantial contributions later in your career. For all of these reasons, you should avoid tampering with your retirement fund if at all possible.

In order to decrease the chance that you might have to invade your retirement fund, most financial planners suggest that you build up a cash hoard equal to between three and six months' salary in order to cope with an emergency. In reality, few people have the ability to build up an emergency fund while also saving for their children's education and their retirement. What are your options if you are forced to tap into your retirement funds?

One solution is to borrow against your fund. Recent surveys indicate that 80% of employers include a loan provision in their plan, and one-third of the remainder expect to do so in the near future. Typically, you can borrow up to 50% of the value of your vested assets with a minimum loan of $1,000. Most important, no tax penalty will be assessed on your loan as long as you make principal and interest payments when they are due. Assuming that your plan does not contain a loan provision, under what circumstances can you gain access to your funds?

While your employer has the right to impose additional restrictions, you normally may withdraw funds as follows:

- At retirement
- Upon attainment of age $59\frac{1}{2}$
- Assuming disability or death
- Upon separation from service
- In the case of hardship

The hardship provision requires an immediate financial need for which funds are not reasonably available from other resources of the employee. For 401(k) and 403(b) plans, the following circumstances qualify as immediate financial needs:

- Unforeseen medical expenses
- Purchase of a principal residence
- The potential loss of a principal residence due to foreclosure or eviction
- Payment of college tuition

In the case of 457 plans, purchase of a residence and the payment of college tuition do not qualify for the hardship withdrawal provision.

Withdrawals from your plan will also subject you to a significant tax liability, because the entire amount of the withdrawal will be taxed as ordinary income during the current year. Moreover, any withdrawals made prior to age $59\frac{1}{2}$ will be subject to an additional tax surcharge of 10%.

The existence of these restrictions and penalties should lead you to two important conclusions. First, retirement plans are not designed as temporary savings vehicles, and you should try to meet any unforeseen cash needs from other sources of funds. Second, if you must tap into your retirement account, a loan represents the least costly option in most circumstances.

WHAT HAPPENS TO YOUR RETIREMENT FUND IF YOU CHANGE EMPLOYERS?

IRS regulations generally make it very easy to transfer your retirement fund to another vehicle if you change employers.

As was mentioned above, you *do* have the option to withdraw your funds at that time, but you will be subject to both ordinary income tax and the 10% penalty. Therefore, you should transfer your assets to another retirement vehicle if at all possible.

Two options are available. First, if your new employer offers the same type of plan, you may be able to transfer your accumulated balance. This is a convenient solution, because your retirement assets will be concentrated in one place. In fact, this is the sole alternative for 457 plans, which can be moved only to a similar plan at a different employer. The other alternative is to transfer your funds to an IRA Rollover Account, which you can open with a mutual fund group, bank, or other financial services organization. You are not allowed to transfer retirement funds to an existing Individual Retirement Account (IRA) but must create a new account specifically for this distribution. In order to avoid 20% mandatory withholding, you instruct your former employer to transfer your funds directly to the IRA Rollover account. In other words, you are not allowed to personally receive the funds and then transfer them to the Rollover account.

CAN YOU MOVE MONEY FROM ONE INVESTMENT OPTION TO ANOTHER?

Government regulations do not prohibit you from transferring your funds among different investment options, except that you are allowed to move your money only to a vehicle that is approved under your retirement plan. In order to provide employees with a great deal of flexibility, many employers offer a wide array of investment options from several different mutual fund and insurance companies. However, some employers limit employees to monthly or less frequent transfers. Additionally, there may be significant costs involved in changing investments. Specifically, some mutual funds levy a charge against a shareholder's account when shares are redeemed, and most insurance companies assess a surrender charge when an individual withdraws funds.

Chapter 7 examines the cost of investing in some detail. It is recommended that you carefully consider sales and surrender charges when selecting new investment options. If your existing investment vehicles entail surrender charges, you should be very careful about switching funds, because any potential return advantage offered by the new fund may be consumed by the transaction costs.

WHEN ARE YOU REQUIRED TO WITHDRAW FUNDS FROM YOUR RETIREMENT PLAN?

If you or your spouse choose to continue working past age 65, you may not need to draw on your retirement fund for several years. Should you postpone the date on which you begin to receive benefits, your retirement benefit for the remainder of your life is likely to substantially increase, because your fund will enjoy several additional years of tax deferred growth.

For example, an individual who begins drawing benefits at age 70 can expect almost 50% more income than someone who elects to retire at the normal age of 65. However, the IRS requires that benefit payments begin by April 1 following the calendar year in which the participant reaches the age of $70\frac{1}{2}$. In certain cases, distributions may be postponed until an employee's actual retirement date if that occurs after age $70\frac{1}{2}$. Moreover, payments must be at least equal to a minimum amount that is established by the IRS based on each individual's life expectancy, and a 50% tax penalty is applied to the amount by which actual distributions fall short of the minimum. Historically, the IRS has imposed a 15% tax on distributions from retirement plans in excess of $150,000 per annum. However, this penalty has been waived for 1997–1999. Therefore, you should consult with your advisers to see if a change in your withdrawal strategy is appropriate.

WHAT ARE YOUR OPTIONS AT RETIREMENT?

As was mentioned at the outset, a participant in a defined contribution plan must make three key decisions. First she must decide how much to contribute to her retirement fund. Second, she is responsible for allocating her dollars among the various investment vehicles that are available. Finally, at retirement, she must also select from the large number of options available. While the first two decisions garner most of the discussion in retirement planning books (including this one), the third is equally important. In fact, a poor decision at retirement can be disastrous!

The remainder of this chapter focuses on the primary retirement income options and evaluates their pros and cons. However, you should again seek professional counsel to ensure that you make the right decision given your particular circumstances.

Before examining specific options, you should consider your retirement objectives. In addition, you need to evaluate your skills as a money manager and focus on the amount of time that you are willing to commit to handling your affairs during retirement. All of these factors will influence your final decision as to the best income option.

KEY CONSIDERATIONS IN SELECTING A RETIREMENT INCOME OPTION

First, you will need to consider your income needs during retirement. For example, if you have other sources of income that are sufficient to meet the majority of your needs, you may want to minimize the withdrawals from your retirement plan, which will enhance the value of your estate. At the other extreme, an individual with pressing financial needs is allowed to withdraw his entire balance at retirement. Of course, the total value of the withdrawal will be taxable in that year.

An important component of the evaluation of your income needs should be the potential impact of an increase in the cost of living. Some income options provide inflation protection in return for a lower initial level of income, while others provide a higher level that does not increase over time.

Similarly, you will need to take into account the income needs of any dependents. Once again, some options provide income for both your life and that of your surviving spouse. Since there is no such thing as a free lunch, this protection comes at the expense of the level of income that you receive.

A related issue is your health. If you have reason to believe that you will not live to a ripe old age, then you may want to select an option that provides a high level of income for a shorter period of time. On the other hand, if you come from a family of nonagenarians, you will want to ensure that your income stream does not run out.

Another important consideration is the size of the estate that you would like to pass on to your heirs. If you choose an option that provides a high level of current income, you are likely to deplete your assets by the time of your death. In particular, a single life annuity provides no residual benefit to your estate in return for the guarantee of a high level of income for life. On the other hand, various income options are designed to provide some income during your life and a death benefit as well.

Finally, you need to decide whether you want to play an active role in the management of your retirement affairs. If you want to minimize your involvement, you can enter into a contract with an insurance company in which you are guaranteed a certain level of income for life. In this case, you can devote all of your energy to your golf game, because your financial affairs will be largely taken care of. At the other extreme, you can assume responsibility for managing your investments and dole out income to yourself according to a schedule that you establish.

A theme that will be repeated frequently in this book is that every decision involves trade-offs, and that the key to success is to find the right balance. During your career, you will have to find the right balance between risk and return in your investments. When you reach retirement, you will seek the best balance between current income, inflation protection, longevity, and the value of your estate. With these general thoughts in mind, let's turn to an evaluation of specific income options.

RETIREMENT OPTIONS

The most straightforward option of all is to do nothing at retirement. Assuming that you do not require income for a period of time, you may be allowed to leave your assets in your retirement plan, where they will continue to grow on a tax deferred basis. As was previously mentioned, you will be required to withdraw funds shortly after age $70\frac{1}{2}$. But, in the meantime, you can maintain flexibility until you develop a retirement strategy. At any time, you will be free to select one of the remaining options that we will cover. Maintaining your existing fund makes good sense if you are comfortable with the investment vehicles that you are currently using.

If your employer does not allow you to remain in the plan or you wish to move to different investment vehicles, you can transfer your funds to an IRA Rollover account. As was discussed above, you can establish such an account at a financial institution and instruct your former employer to transfer the funds directly. Chapter 7 is devoted to selecting mutual funds and other types of investment vehicles, but it might be helpful to provide a very brief preview here.

When evaluating firms for an IRA Rollover, you should consider the overall reputation of the organization, the variety of investment products offered, the firm's administrative capability, the variety of income options available, and the investment results achieved in its funds. Once you establish an IRA

Rollover, you have considerable flexibility to manage your funds and withdraw income as required. However, you will be assuming a good deal of the responsibility for managing your financial affairs. While your funds are invested in the Rollover account, your assets will continue to grow on a tax deferred basis and you will be taxed only on the distributions that you receive. Once again, the rules regarding minimum distributions after age $70\frac{1}{2}$ apply.

A third option is to take a **lump sum distribution**. In other words, you withdraw the entire balance of your retirement plan. The primary advantage of a lump sum distribution is that it provides you with considerable flexibility. You can use your money for medical expenses, a retirement home, or any other need. Alternatively, you can invest it for future growth. However, the disadvantages of a lump sum generally outweigh the added flexibility. The entire amount of the distribution will be taxed during the current year, and you may be forced into a higher tax bracket because of the one-time surge in income. In certain circumstances, you may also be subject to the 20% withholding requirement or to a tax penalty. Additionally, you may be forced to pay the surrender charge that is levied by some investment vehicles when funds are withdrawn. Most important, you will be assuming complete responsibility for your financial security during retirement. If you don't do a good job of managing your affairs, you could find yourself strapped for cash in the last years of your life. For all of these reasons, lump sum distributions should be avoided unless you have a very pressing financial need that cannot be met through other resources.

The three options considered above were focused on the management of your retirement fund. Now, we turn to the various methods of receiving income from your accumulated assets.

First, many retirement plans allow you to make partial or periodic withdrawals. In other words, you simply withdraw funds from your retirement plan when you need them. Your remaining assets stay invested in the plan and earn a tax deferred rate of return. This option offers considerable flexibility and is designed for those who have other sources of income, to which withdrawals from the retirement plan are used as a supplement. Additionally, depending upon actual withdrawals, you may have a balance in your account upon your death that may be passed on to your heirs. The primary drawback of this approach is that it does not result in a guaranteed source of income, because you can make withdrawals only to the extent that you have funds remaining in the plan. Once your assets are depleted, you are out of luck!

A related approach involves systematic withdrawals. In this case, you instruct the organization holding your retirement assets to make regular payments to you at a level that you select. Once again, these payments continue only as long as you have assets in the plan and are not guaranteed in any way. With both of these options, the size of your withdrawals and the return that you earn on the assets remaining in the plan will determine how long the payments last. Don't forget, each withdrawal will be subject to ordinary income tax, and you also run the risk of a severe tax penalty if you do not meet the minimum distribution requirements imposed by the IRS.

All of the options that we have considered entail financial risk or require some effort on your part. If you find a simple and safe option more appealing, an annuity may fit the bill.

AN OVERVIEW OF ANNUITIES

An annuity is a contract with an insurance company in which the company agrees to pay you income for a designated period of time. While there are dozens of different types of annuities, they fall under two broad categories: **fixed** and **variable**.

A **fixed** annuity represents a promise to pay you a specific amount of money for a designated period of time. For instance, you might purchase an annuity in which the company is obligated to pay you $1,000 per month for the remainder of your life. The key to a fixed annuity is that the payment is based on an assumed rate of return that is fixed for the life of the contract and the cost of the annuity contract is paid up front. The critical point is that the insurance company assumes the risk of poor investment performance. When an individual purchases a fixed annuity, the up-front payment is generally invested by the insurance company in a variety of fixed income securities.

In contrast, the payment under a **variable** annuity contract depends upon the actual investment returns that are earned. In this case, the individual has the ability to choose among a number of different investment options, including the insurance company's own portfolios and mutual funds that are made available through the variable annuity program. The initial income payment under a variable annuity is based on an assumed rate of return, and subsequent payments are based on the actual returns on the vehicles the individual selects.

In general, fixed annuities are appropriate for people who want a stable and predictable level of income and no investment responsibility. Variable annuities offer the opportunity to earn higher rates of return through the use of equities and other more aggressive investments that are normally not included in fixed annuity portfolios. However, a variable annuity requires the participant to make some investment decisions, and the potential exists that annuity payments will be below those offered by fixed products.

An ideal solution for many people is a blend of fixed and variable annuities. The fixed annuity provides stable and predictable income, while the variable annuity offers the potential for higher return and protection against inflation.

ANNUITY PRODUCT DESCRIPTIONS

An exhaustive description of annuities might fill this entire book and would certainly provide a cure for insomnia. Therefore, coverage will be limited to a few of the more popular options.

The most straightforward alternative is the **single life annuity,** which provides guaranteed income for the duration of one individual's life. The price of an annuity of this sort is based on the individual's life expectancy and the assumed rate of return on the up-front payment. Should the annuitant outlive his life expectancy, the insurance company is obligated to continue to make payments even though it may lose money on this particular contract. But, by issuing a large number of annuities, the company can assume that the life expectancy assumptions will prove correct in aggregate.

The primary advantage of this option is simplicity. There are two disadvantages. First, the contract terminates at the death of the individual and there is no residual payment to his estate. Should he die prematurely, the annuity will have represented a poor investment. Second, this form of annuity does not provide ongoing income for a surviving spouse.

Both of these drawbacks can be eliminated, although there is some cost involved. First, insurance companies offer a single life annuity with a guaranteed payment option. For example, you might select an annuity with twenty years of guaranteed payments. If you die during the twenty-year period, the remaining payments will be made to your designated beneficiary or to your estate. If you live for more than twenty years, your payments will continue until death. The cost of this guarantee feature is a lower payment than you would receive under the simple annuity structure. The second drawback leads many people to select a **joint-and-survivor** annuity, which pays income for the life of an individual and a surviving spouse or dependent. In fact, this option is required under certain plans. A joint-and-survivor annuity can be structured to provide constant payments over both lives. Alternatively, the payment to the survivor can be lower than the initial payment, based on the assumption that one person can live more frugally than two.

A **designated period** annuity provides a specific payment for a designated period of time. For example, you might choose to receive $1,000 per month for twenty-five years. Because this option does not place the insurance company at risk should you outlive your life expectancy, you will receive a higher payment than some other options would provide. On the other hand, if you live longer than twenty-five years, you are up a creek without a paddle.

A **unit refund life** annuity pays you income for life and then returns any remaining capital in your account to your estate upon your death. This alternative makes sense for individuals who are particularly interested in providing funds to heirs.

Finally, a single life annuity with **inflation protection** provides income for life with an upward adjustment in the annual payment to offset the rising cost of living. Typically, you are allowed to select the amount by which the payment increases every year within a range of 2% to 6%, which should represent plenty of protection except in extreme circumstances. Of course, the initial payment will be lower than that provided by a plain vanilla annuity, and the amount of the penalty depends upon the size of the inflation adjustment. Despite the lower initial payment, inflation protection is a very valuable option that most people should consider.

WHERE IS THE ASPIRIN BOTTLE?

By this point, all of these options may have given you a major headache! Retirement planning is a complex topic and can at times seem overwhelming. It is strongly recommended that you work closely with your employer and any outside advisers. However, the information contained in this chapter should provide you with enough background to focus on the critical issues and ask the right questions. Once you get your retirement plan established, the process of investing your money will be a lot easier and more interesting.

Key Points to Remember

- The amount that you can contribute to your retirement plan is governed by IRS regulations and any restrictions imposed by your employer.

- You should not use your plan as a temporary savings vehicle because of restrictions on withdrawals and tax penalties.

- At retirement, you should select an income option after considering your income needs, inflation, and the necessity to protect a spouse or dependents.

CHAPTER 3

How Much Should You Contribute to Your Retirement Plan?

Failing to prepare is like preparing to fail.

—JOHN WOODEN

Saving money for your future certainly isn't as much fun as buying a new car or taking a vacation! On the other hand, can you imagine spending the "golden years" of your life worrying about how to make ends meet? The challenge in retirement planning is to achieve a balance between now and the future—to enjoy the working portion of your life while also providing for your retirement years. It won't always be easy, and you will have to make some sacrifices along the way. However, the information included in this book should get you off to a good start and help you determine a target level of savings that will meet your future needs. At that point, it will be up to you to take the first step.

WHY YOU CAN'T AFFORD TO WAIT

The clock is ticking! As the example in Chapter 1 demonstrated, the longer you wait to begin your savings program, the more difficult it will be to achieve your retirement objectives. And, at some point, it will become impossible to catch up.

While you may not think that you can afford to save, the reality is that you cannot afford *not* to save. Getting started is important even if you are not saving at the ideal level. Continuing with the example from Chapter 1, in which our subject had a target level of saving 10% of her salary, suppose she is able to put aside only 5% during each of the first five years. During the remainder of her career, she need only save 11.6% annually in order to accomplish her original objective. With a little bit of belt tightening, this goal seems reasonably attainable. Don't forget, these savings rates represent the total amount of money that should be contributed to a retirement plan. After taking into account her employer's matching funds, her contribution should be very manageable.

THE BENEFITS OF TAX DEFERRAL

Retirement plans represent one of the most attractive ways to save due to the power of tax deferral. Tax deferral refers to the fact that most contributions to retirement plans represent pre-tax dollars and no tax is payable on a retirement plan as it grows. Instead, taxes are deferred until you begin to receive retirement income, and this deferral can have a major impact on the ultimate size of your fund.

Assume, for example, that you are able to devote $2,000 per year of your income to a savings program. If this saving takes place outside of a retirement plan, you will first have to pay tax on your income, which will amount to $560 assuming a 28% tax rate. Therefore, only $1,440 is actually invested in the savings program. Moreover, you will have to pay tax on the interest that your investment earns. Assuming a 7% return, the 28% tax reduces the net return to 5%. Over thirty years, an annual contribution of $1,440 earning 5% will result in an ultimate value of $95,672.

In contrast, by contributing the $2,000 to a retirement plan, the entire amount would be invested and you would earn the full 7% return. At the end of thirty years, your retirement plan would be worth $188,922, which represents a 97% increase over the first example! That is the power of tax deferral. Another way of looking at its power is that participation in the retirement plan allows you to save $2,000 at a cost of only $1,440 due to the tax saving.

As was discussed in Chapter 2, there may be some restrictions on withdrawals from retirement plans, and any withdrawal may trigger unpleasant tax consequences. For both of these reasons, a retirement plan should not be used as a temporary saving vehicle. But most, if not all, of the savings that you designate for retirement should be directed to retirement plans in order to capture the power of tax deferral. The remainder of this chapter is devoted to helping you figure out how much you should contribute to your retirement plan, and the focus will be on the minimum amount necessary to achieve your goals. However, after reading the section on the power of tax deferral, you may be motivated to maximize your contribution. If so, you should review the section in Chapter 2 that discusses the maximum limits on contributions imposed by the IRS.

HOW MUCH INCOME WILL YOU NEED DURING RETIREMENT?

In order to determine how much money you need to accumulate over the course of your career, you must first estimate the amount of income that you will require during retirement.

There are two approaches to estimating retirement income needs. The first is the more exact method, which requires you to list all of your current living expenses and to identify those that will continue after retirement. For example, you probably will have paid off your mortgage by that time, but real estate taxes and insurance will continue. Any expenses related to your job will stop at retirement, but you will assume new expenses, including health care, travel, and recreation. Once you identify all of the categories that will continue, you add up the amount that you would spend in each category, assuming that you were retired today. This sum is then adjusted for taxes and inflation in order to estimate the amount of income that you will need at your future retirement date. Finally, this figure can be translated into the amount that you should save along the way to have sufficient assets at retirement. This method involves some research on your part, as well as a good bit of number crunching.

Thankfully, your employer's Human Resources department probably has a computer program to assist in this process. If not, software is also available from most mutual fund companies for a very nominal price. Finally, if you want some personalized assistance, a financial planner will be glad to guide you through the process for a fee.

The second method of estimating retirement income is a shortcut that requires you to make only one simple decision. Financial planners have coined the phrase "replacement ratio" to refer to the amount of income that you will need during retirement as a percentage of your salary immediately prior to retirement. Stated another way, your retirement plan is designed to "replace" the income that your job provided before retirement. As a rule, people find that they need modestly less income during retirement because of the absence of work-related expenses such as clothing, commuting costs, and the like. Therefore, most experts recommend that your retirement income represent between 60% and 90% of your income immediately prior to retirement. For example, you should plan on income of $18,000 to $27,000 assuming a salary during the last year of your career of $30,000. Obviously, $18,000 to $27,000, or a replacement ratio of 60% to 90%, is a very large range, so what should you actually shoot for?

The replacement ratio that is right for you depends on your personal situation and on the kind of lifestyle you plan to lead during retirement. Let's consider your personal circumstances first. If you have a low-to-medium level of income, then there is relatively little slack in your budget; most of your income is required just to cover the basic necessities of life. In your case, there will be very little change in your income needs during retirement, so you should shoot for a replacement ratio of 90% or even higher. On the other hand, higher-income individuals have excess income that can be devoted to investments, charity, and gifts to family members. In their case, the actual cost of living consumes a smaller percentage of their income, which means that they can get by with a much lower replacement ratio.

The other critical issue is the lifestyle that you prefer. If you plan to take up expensive hobbies or travel extensively during retirement, then a high ratio is appropriate. In fact, some people shoot for a replacement ratio greater than 100%, because they want to be able to do all of the things that they never had time for during their careers. At the other extreme, a ratio of 60% or so will probably do if you plan to putter around the house. Another issue to keep in mind is that many retirees now choose to take part-time jobs. While they are not always motivated by the money involved, a little extra income will allow for a lower replacement ratio.

There are no simple guidelines or rules of thumb that will tell you which ratio is right for you. However, a high ratio (80% or 90%) is advisable for a couple of reasons. First, a high target will provide you with the discipline and motivation to maintain your program. Second, given the potential for rising costs during retirement, it is better to overestimate your needs. Finally, as long as you begin saving early in your career, high ratios are within your grasp, so why not aim for the highest possible living standard?

INTEGRATING SOCIAL SECURITY

As was mentioned in Chapter 1, there are serious questions regarding the outlook for the Social Security system, and it is very possible that baby boomers will not receive the benefits that have been promised. Therefore, the most conservative approach to retirement planning is to assume that your personal savings will have to provide all of your retirement income. If you want to make that assumption, you can skip to the next section.

Assuming that Social Security does survive in its current form, how do you integrate it into your retirement planning? In simple terms, any income that you receive from Social Security will reduce the amount that you have to replace with your own retirement savings. How much can you expect to receive from Social Security? Unfortunately, the Social Security benefit formula is very complicated, since it takes into account your annual salary, the number of years worked, inflation, and a variety of other factors. Therefore, it is difficult to calculate your benefit directly. But by contacting your local Social Security office, you can follow the procedures necessary for the agency to estimate the benefit for you. Your Human Resources department may be able to calculate an estimate as well, and most financial software packages have a built-in Social Security function.

As a shortcut, place yourself in one of the following income groups:

Group 1.	Income today of $20,000 or less
Group 2.	Income of $20,000 to $50,000
Group 3.	Income of $50,000 to $80,000
Group 4.	Income of $80,000 or more

The following provides an indication of the amount of income that will be replaced by Social Security:

Group 1.   60%

Group 2.   40%

Group 3.   20%

Group 4.   10%

The appropriate percentage should be subtracted from your target replacement ratio in order to determine the amount of retirement income that must be provided by your retirement plan. For example, after considering her desired standard of living during retirement, an individual with a salary of $30,000 selects a target replacement ratio of 90%. In other words, she wants retirement income equal to 90% of her salary during the last year of her career. The above tables suggest that about 40% of her final salary will be provided by Social Security, which means that her own savings must supply 50% (90% - 40%). In the next section, that 50% net target will be translated into an appropriate level of annual saving.

While this section is devoted to integrating Social Security, you should also make an adjustment for any other sources of retirement income. For example, you may be entitled to receive a pension from a previous job or from military service. You should consult with your employer's Human Resources or Benefits departments to properly evaluate benefits of this type.

HOW MUCH SHOULD YOU SAVE TOWARD RETIREMENT?

At this point, you should have selected a target replacement ratio and adjusted it for the Social Security benefits that you expect to receive. The next step is to focus on the following table in order to determine what percentage of your income should be contributed to your retirement plan. This table is based on "middle-of-the-road" assumptions regarding the return that you will earn on your retirement fund and the rate at which your salary will grow throughout your career. Additionally, it is designed for a couple who are approximately the same age and assumes that retirement income will be necessary for both of their lives.

Table 3.1
DETERMINING A SAVINGS RATE

	YEARS UNTIL RETIREMENT						
	40	35	30	25	20	15	10
120	17	22	30	41	59	90	153
110	15	20	27	38	54	82	140
100	14	18	25	34	49	75	127
90	12	16	22	31	44	67	115
80	11	15	20	27	39	60	102
70	10	13	17	24	34	52	89
60	8	11	15	20	29	45	76
50	7	9	12	17	25	37	64
40	6	7	10	14	20	30	51
30	4	5	7	10	15	22	38
20	3	4	5	7	10	15	25
10	1	2	2	3	5	7	13

REPLACEMENT RATIO (%)

First, move across the top of the table until you find the number of years until your planned retirement date. Then, focus on the left-hand column to identify your target replacement ratio after adjusting for the impact of Social Security. The intersecting box tells you the percentage of your salary that you should contribute annually to your retirement fund. For example, suppose an individual with thirty years until retirement wants to replace 90% of his income. He assumes that Social Security will replace 40% of his income, which means that his retirement savings must replace 50%. The intersecting box indicates that he should be contributing 12% of salary.

At first blush, the required savings percentages in this table look pretty scary. However, these percentages represent the total amount that should be contributed to a fund. If your retirement plan includes a matching provision, then your personal contribution should be much more manageable. For example, many companies match their employees' contributions dollar for dollar, which would call for only a 6% contribution by the employee in the above example. You should also recall that the table is designed for a couple. If you are single, a lower savings rate will probably be sufficient.

The savings rates in Table 3.1 also assume that you are starting from scratch and have accumulated no assets up to this point. If you have already built up a nest egg, the job will be a good bit easier. The next table (Table 3.2) helps you adjust for the retirement savings that you already have.

Table 3.2
ASSET ADJUSTMENT FACTOR

Years Until Retirement

Ratio Assets/Salary (%)	40	35	30	25	20	15	10
0.2	1	1	1	1	2	2	3
0.4	2	2	3	3	3	4	5
0.6	4	4	4	4	5	6	8
0.8	5	5	5	6	7	8	11
1.0	6	6	7	7	8	10	13
1.2	7	7	8	9	10	12	16
1.4	8	9	9	10	11	14	19
1.6	9	10	11	12	13	16	21
1.8	11	11	12	13	15	18	24
2.0	12	12	13	14	16	20	27
2.2	13	14	15	16	18	22	29
2.4	14	15	16	17	20	24	32
2.6	15	16	17	19	21	26	35
2.8	17	17	19	20	23	28	37
3.0	18	19	20	22	25	30	40

First, add up the value of all of your retirement funds and then divide this sum by your annual salary. For example, suppose that the subject in the example accompanying the previous table had managed to accumulate $18,000 in his retirement plan. If you divide this sum by his annual salary of

$30,000, you get a ratio of 0.6. Locate this figure in the left-hand column of the table. Then move across until you reach the column representing thirty years remaining until his retirement date. The number in the intersecting box (4%) should be subtracted from the 12% savings rate found in the previous table. Therefore, our saver can reduce his 12% savings rate to 8% because of the assets he has already put aside. If his employer matches one-for-one, he will be able to get by with as little as a 4% personal contribution. If your required savings rate is zero or negative after adjusting for your existing assets, then you already have sufficient funds to meet your retirement needs.

You should now have figured out your target level of contribution to your retirement plan. Don't be discouraged! If the numbers seem unreachable, remember that this is the average amount that you should save during the remainder of your career. Get started even if your initial savings rate is below the required level, because you can always exceed the target in later years once the children leave the nest and you have more discretionary income.

STRATEGIES FOR GETTING STARTED

It's all well and good to talk about the importance of saving, but how do you get started when you probably feel that your budget is already stretched to the limit? Unfortunately, there is no painless way to save, but there are a few simple steps that will minimize the impact on your current living standard.

The basic idea is that you save any dollars that are not already built into your daily budget. For example, income tax withholding tables are designed so that most people receive tax refunds in April of each year. Why not contribute your refund to your retirement plan? After all, you have been living throughout the year on your salary, so the tax refund should represent "found money." The same principle applies to a bonus or profit-sharing distribution that you receive from your employer. Once again, if you have managed your living standard to your income, those dollars can be allocated to savings without having an impact on your lifestyle. Finally, a great way to get started is to "save your annual raise." Suppose that your annual salary is $30,000 and that you are awarded a 5% salary increase. If you devote the entire $1,500 raise to your retirement program, your lifestyle should stay about the same, because you were living on $30,000 anyway. In reality, your living standard will decrease a bit, because inflation will raise the cost of everything you buy while your income stays the same. But this strategy of forgoing your raise is a one-time step. Once you establish your saving routine, any future raises can be used to enhance your living standard.

Most people feel that their budget is pretty tight, but in fact, virtually everyone has at least a few discretionary dollars. Make the tough decision to save some of those dollars. Remember, the key is to achieve the right balance between enjoying life today and preparing for your future.

THE WORLD OF INVESTMENTS

The next four chapters are devoted to helping you make good investment decisions within your retirement funds. In fact, your success as an investor will have a major impact on the amount of money that you have to contribute to your fund.

As previously mentioned, the tables included in this chapter were based on "middle-of-the-road" investment returns. If your actual return exceeds the assumption by 1%, you will be able to reduce your contribution by about 3% of salary. Alternatively, you can maintain your contribution and enjoy a higher standard of living during retirement.

Key Points to Remember

- Most people should shoot for a replacement ratio of 80% to 90%.

- After adjusting for Social Security, use Tables 3.1 and 3.2 to determine how much of your income should be contributed to your retirement fund.

- Begin saving even if you are unable to contribute at the target level.

CHAPTER 4

A Primer on Investments

Too much of a good thing is wonderful.

—MAE WEST

Mae West's clever quip certainly applies to some facets of life, but the variety of investments available to even the smallest investor is not one of them.

Unfortunately, every investor is deluged with information about stocks, bonds, money market funds, commodities, and dozens of other investment products. How in the world can anyone understand all of these alternatives, much less choose among them? Most 401(k), 403(b), and similar retirement plans offer at least four or five different investment categories, and it is not unusual to find plans that offer dozens of alternatives including very specialized and exotic strategies. Additionally, many plans offer the opportunity to switch among funds as often as every day. Do you really need all of this flexibility?

The simple answer is no. By dividing your money among four or five carefully selected categories and maintaining your weightings over time, you should enjoy an attractive rate of return and an acceptable level of risk. This chapter provides descriptions of the basic investment categories that should be found in most retirement plans. Chapters 5 and 6 provide a great deal of information on various combinations of these investments, and they help you select the combination that best meets your needs. Finally, Chapter 7 focuses on selecting specific mutual funds and insurance products for each category of investment.

MUTUAL FUNDS AND ANNUITIES

Before turning to specific investments, it might be helpful to briefly discuss mutual funds and annuities, since they represent the vehicles through which most retirement investors access the financial world.

A **mutual fund** is simply a legal entity in which numerous investors pool their money in order to invest more efficiently. By joining other investors, an individual gains access to professional management and removes most of the headaches associated with record keeping and tax preparation. More important, participation in a pool provides an investor with a great deal more diversification than he could achieve on his own. Finally, mutual funds are highly regulated by the Securities and Exchange Commission, which provides investors with the assurance that their money is being handled prudently.

More than 6,000 mutual funds are currently offered to investors in the United States, and every conceivable security or strategy is represented in one or more of them. One problem that you will face in selecting mutual funds is that the stated objective of a fund and the investment strategy that it follows are not always clear and in agreement. For example, "growth" is a common objective for mutual funds, yet the strategies implemented by growth funds vary significantly. Therefore, it is important that you gain a basic understanding of the types of securities in which mutual funds invest.

As was discussed in Chapter 2, an annuity is a contract with an insurance company in which the company promises to make payments for a specified period. At retirement, many people purchase an annuity in order to have a predictable income stream. However, an annuity can also be used as the vehicle to accumulate funds for retirement. In this instance, the individual makes contributions to the insurance company during her career and then selects from a variety of distribution options at retirement. Contributions to annuities are either invested directly by the insurance company or allocated to a variety of mutual funds as selected by the employee.

AN INTRODUCTION TO FINANCE

While each type of investment has unique features and many are rather complex, most securities actually fit into one of two very basic categories: **debt** or **equity**. Let's explore each of these, with particular emphasis on the way in which an investor earns a return.

Broadly defined, an **equity** is any investment in which the purchaser assumes an ownership position in something. The most common example is a share of stock in a company. If you purchase one share of stock in a company that has a total of one hundred outstanding shares, you own 1% of the company. In reality, most companies have millions of shares of outstanding stock, so any single investor generally owns only a small fraction of 1%. However, the principle is the same. While the words *stocks* and *equities* are often used interchangeably, there are many types of "equity" investments in addition to stocks. Other examples include the purchase of a parcel of real estate or ownership in an oil or gas well.

The return that you earn as an equity owner comes from two sources: **current income** and **appreciation**. Each component of return can be evaluated using stocks as an example.

First, many companies pay out a portion of their earnings to shareholders in the form of dividends, which are generally paid quarterly. For example, a company might pay out an annual dividend of $1.00, which means that each shareholder receives a quarterly check of $.25 for each share owned. While companies are occasionally forced to cut their dividend due to a decline in profits, dividends usually represent a stable and predictable source of return. Since 1926, the average company has paid an annual dividend equal to 4.6% of its stock price. In other words, a shareholder received a 4.6% return on her investment before taking into account any change in the price of her stock. Currently, the dividend yield on the Standard and Poors 500 is only about 1.4%, which means that appreciation will likely constitute a greater portion of total return. While the average company pays a dividend, corporations that are growing very rapidly generally do not, because they are able to reinvest their earnings in the business. Therefore, mutual funds that concentrate in rapidly growing companies usually pay lower dividends than other types of stock funds. Additionally, many companies repurchase their own shares in the market rather than pay cash dividends to shareholders. While an investor does not receive any current income in this instance, share repurchases generally contribute to rising stock prices, which may be more beneficial over the long pull.

While the dividend is important, the larger component of return is attributable to changes in stock prices. Since 1926, the average stock has appreciated 5.9% per year. When combined with the dividend return of 4.6%, this suggests that stockholders have earned a total annual return of 10.7%. (The 10.7% return does not equal the sum of 4.6% and 5.9% due to the effect of reinvesting dividends and interest.) This return exceeds the performance of most other categories of investment, which is the reason that stocks play an important role in enhancing the return on a retirement fund.

Why do the prices of stocks rise more often than not? Over time, stock prices tend to move in concert with the profits of corporations, which increase as the world economy grows. As a matter of fact, growth in U.S. corporate profits since 1926 has exactly equaled the 5.9% annual appreciation on stocks. Over shorter periods, stock prices fluctuate around the trend in corporate profits, because investors frequently change their view as to how much they are willing to pay for future growth. For example, during periods of low inflation and stable interest rates, investors are generally willing to pay more for a given company's stock even though the prospects for that company may not have changed. Of course, investors sometimes become cautious, which leads to declining prices. While stocks have earned an average return of 10.7% during the past seventy-one years, it is important that you understand that the actual return in any given year has ranged from 54% to negative 43%. However, don't be put off by the 43% decline! Serious declines in stock prices are fairly rare, and long-term investors have plenty of time to recover from a temporary market setback. Later, we will evaluate historical return data on stocks in some detail.

The other major category of investments includes bonds, money market securities, and a variety of other **debt instruments.** Whereas a stock represents ownership in a company, a bond or similar instrument represents a loan to a company (or to the U.S. Government). Suppose you purchase a five-year U.S. Treasury Bond that pays an interest rate of 7%. In reality, you are loaning $1,000 to the U.S. Government, which promises to pay you annual interest of $70 and to return your $1,000 at the end of five years. Similarly, when you purchase a Certificate of Deposit, or CD, from a bank, you are loaning the bank money that it in turn lends to other customers. The bank earns a profit by charging borrowers a higher interest rate than it pays on CDs.

The return on a debt instrument is largely a function of its interest rate if held to maturity. As the above example demonstrates, if you purchase and hold a U.S. Government bond, you are assured of receiving both interest and principal on the scheduled payment dates. However, should you sell a bond prior to its maturity, it is possible that you will experience a gain or loss in addition to the interest payment. For example, if you purchase the Treasury bond mentioned above for $1,000 but are forced to sell it for $900 after two years, the $100 capital loss offsets most of the $140 in interest that was earned.

Why do bond prices decline at times? Suppose market interest rates rise to 8% shortly after you purchase a Treasury bond that pays 7%. Why would any investor be interested in purchasing your 7% bond when he could purchase a newly issued bond that pays 8%? In order to induce him to purchase your bond, you will have to sell it at a discount. Specifically, at a price of $974, your 7% bond will provide the same return as the 8% bond purchased at $1,000. Bond prices fall during periods of rising interest rates and rise when rates are falling. However, changes in bond prices tend to be more moderate than stock price fluctuations, and bonds usually offer lower rates of return.

It is important that you understand that holding a bond mutual fund is different from owning a bond directly. As mentioned above, buying and holding an individual bond provides a predictable stream of payments and an assured return. But mutual funds constantly buy and sell bonds, which means that they realize gains and losses in addition to interest income. Therefore, your return as a shareholder in the fund is not guaranteed in any way and can fluctuate with changes in interest rates. A risk to holders of some types of debt instruments is that the borrower is unable to make interest and principal payments due to financial weakness. However, this risk is minuscule for high-quality corporate borrowers and the U.S. Government.

In summary, the prices of both bonds and stocks fluctuate over time, but the return on bonds is a little more stable because interest payments represent the bulk of their return. With these general comments in mind, the next section contains a more detailed discussion of various types of stocks and bonds.

STOCKS

If you have tried to follow the stock market, you have probably been overwhelmed by the variety of stocks that seems to be available. Among the categories that are often mentioned are blue chip stocks, growth stocks, value stocks, small stocks, income stocks, foreign stocks, mid-cap stocks, and so on.

In reality, only three stock categories are necessary to provide you with a well-structured program, and all three are now available in most 401(k) plans. They are **large capitalization stocks**, **small capitalization stocks**, and **foreign stocks**. As was mentioned above, you will have to evaluate the mutual funds offered by your plan in order to select those that concentrate on these categories. Of course, you should feel free to add other types of funds to your retirement plan, but these three represent the minimum.

Before these categories are described, the word *capitalization* requires definition. The capitalization of a company is calculated by multiplying its stock price by the number of shares outstanding. In other words, it is the value of the entire company in the stock market and is a commonly used measure of size. For example, IBM has approximately 943 million outstanding shares, which results in a market capitalization of $141 billion when multiplied by the current stock price of $150.

The **large capitalization stock** category is generally defined as the 500 largest capitalization stocks that make up the well-known Standard and Poors 500 Stock Index (S&P 500). In addition to IBM, this group includes General Electric, Coca-Cola, Exxon, AT&T, Microsoft, and a number of other blue chip companies. These are the large, dominant companies that represent the backbone of corporate America. Most mainstream stock mutual funds concentrate in large capitalization issues because of their size, liquidity, and the availability of research reports and financial information.

Small capitalization stocks are those with market values of $5 billion or less. Smaller companies are entrepreneurial by nature and are frequently able to adjust more rapidly than larger organizations to changes in the business climate. Moreover, they tend to be concentrated in higher growth industries, such as health care and technology. For both of these reasons, they enjoy more rapid growth in profits than their larger cousins, and this growth has resulted in an annual return to shareholders of 12.6% since 1926 as compared to the 10.7% return on the S&P 500 Index. Because of this return advantage, most "aggressive" stock mutual funds invest heavily in this category, and the return on your retirement plan will be enhanced by allocating some of your money to such a fund.

Why don't investors place most of their money in small stocks? Unfortunately, each type of investment has both strengths and weaknesses, and smaller stocks pose some risks that need to be considered. Smaller companies generally do not enjoy the financial strength of the corporate giants, and some inevitably fail when the economy turns down. While industries such as health care and technology enjoy high growth, they are very competitive, which also results in occasional casualties. As a result of these and other factors, smaller stocks tend to be more volatile than mature companies. In other words, their stock prices tend to rise more during rising markets and fall more during bear markets. For example, small stocks declined by 45% during the severe bear market of 1973–74, as compared to 37% for the blue chips. Finally, the extra return earned by small stocks tends to come in spurts. From 1974 through 1983, small stocks outperformed their larger counterparts only to perform poorly from 1983 through 1990. Therefore, investing in small stocks requires a reasonable degree of patience and a long time horizon.

Foreign stocks are the same in many respects as U.S. securities, except that they are traded on exchanges outside the United States. Why should a U.S. investor allocate funds to foreign stocks? First, foreign stocks constitute approximately 50% of the value of the global stock market. Therefore, an investor who limits himself to U.S. stocks is missing out on 50% of the potential opportunities. Second, many countries enjoy faster economic growth than the United States, which has a relatively mature economy. In general, faster economic growth translates into faster growth in corporate profits and higher returns on stocks. Finally, foreign stock markets do not move in tandem with the U.S. market. For example, while the U.S. market declined by 3.2% in 1990, the Hong Kong and British markets rose 9.2% and 10.3%, respectively. Therefore, a combination of domestic and foreign stocks will fluctuate less than a purely domestic portfolio.

Once again, foreign stocks have several drawbacks. First, they are generally more volatile than their American counterparts. In particular, companies based in smaller, emerging countries experience huge swings in stock price. Second, foreign stocks often entail political risk when they are based in countries with unstable or unfriendly governments. Finally, all foreign stocks involve currency risk, because a U.S. investor must convert dollars to local currency in order to execute trades. Despite these risks, foreign stocks play an important role because of the potential for superior returns and the smoothing effect they have on a domestic retirement fund.

Three different types of mutual funds offer exposure to foreign stocks. First, international stock funds invest in stocks traded on exchanges in the major industrialized countries of Europe and Asia. Emerging stock funds invest in developing countries such as Mexico and Malaysia. Global funds have the greatest flexibility, since they can invest anywhere in the world, including the United States. Unfortunately, these fund categories are often blurred, because fund managers are given a great deal of latitude to invest in any market that they believe is attractive. For example, international funds often allocate as much as 20% of their assets to emerging markets when they are deemed particularly compelling.

Chapter 1 discussed the importance of an organized approach to investing that is designed to deliver both a healthy return and an acceptable level of risk. While this approach is discussed in Chapters 5 and 6, a brief preview might be helpful at this point.

The key to success is to combine a number of different types of securities in your retirement plan, including both stocks and bonds. In the investment world, the process of blending different types of investments is known as **diversification**.

To demonstrate the power of diversification, let's focus on a blend of the three types of stocks that were discussed above. For the twenty years ending in 1995, an investor in large capitalization stocks such as the Standard and Poors 500 earned an annual average return of 14.5%. In contrast, a blend of 45% large capitalization, 30% small capitalization, and 25% foreign stocks earned an annual average return of 16.5%. Additionally, the blended portfolio suffered a negative return in only one of the twenty years as compared to three for the S&P 500. Not only did the annual return increase by an average of 2%, but the blended portfolio was more stable! If there is any "free lunch" in the financial world, this is it.

The Power of Diversification

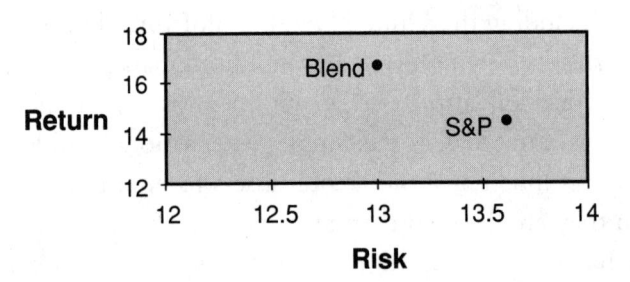

Chart 4.1

This is a chart that is commonly used in the financial world to compare the risk and return on different types of investments, and it graphically demonstrates the point that was made above. The dot representing the blended portfolio is above and to the left of the S&P 500, which means that it delivers more return with less risk. When we add bonds to the picture, the balance between risk and return will improve even further.

BONDS

The stock portion of your retirement plan was designed to achieve high returns, albeit with some volatility. In contrast, bonds provide a predictable source of current income and relative stability. Since 1926, long-term U.S. Government bonds have earned an annual return of 5.7%, as compared to the 10.7% return on stocks. During the past twenty years the spread has been much smaller, as bonds have earned 11.9% per annum as compared to 14.8% for stocks. Looking ahead, it is reasonable to expect that stocks will outperform bonds by 3% to 4% per year.

What about volatility? As mentioned earlier, annual stock returns have ranged between 54% and negative 43% since 1926. In contrast, the worst annual loss on bonds was 9%, while the best year was limited to a positive return of 40%. Clearly, bonds experience smaller price swings than stocks, although the range is still fairly significant. If you want to eliminate price changes entirely, most retirement plans offer at least one bond fund in which the price of the fund stays constant. Not surprisingly, that stability has a cost, which is a lower return.

While bonds seem simple enough on the surface, there are many varieties of debt securities, and they behave quite differently depending upon the direction of interest rates. As mentioned above, the prices of some bonds are fixed, while others fluctuate significantly. Let's examine the types of bond funds that are commonly available in 401(k), 403(b), and 457 retirement plans.

One way to characterize bonds is to focus on the **issuer**. U.S. Government bond mutual funds invest solely in bonds issued by Uncle Sam, which means that the payment of interest and principal is guaranteed by the full faith and credit of the United States government. In contrast, corporate funds invest in bonds issued by corporations. The primary difference between the two is that corporations are occasionally unable to pay interest or principal, resulting in a default. Defaults are quite rare among the blue chips, but they occur more frequently among companies with weak finances. Corporate bonds have historically provided investors with an extra .7% in annual return, as compared to government issues, in order to compensate them for the risk of default. "Junk" (also known as high-yield) bond funds invest in low-quality corporate bonds. Because they are particularly exposed to the risk of default, junk bond interest rates typically exceed the rate on U.S. Treasury issues by 3.5%. Finally, foreign bond funds invest in bonds that are issued by corporations or governments outside of the United States. In addition to the usual risks associated with bonds, foreign issues entail political and currency risk.

A second way to characterize bonds is to focus on **maturity**. Bonds with short maturities pay relatively low coupon or interest rates, but their prices do not fall very much as a result of an increase in the level of rates. In contrast, long-term bonds experience wide swings in price but pay a higher coupon. Once again, we find that every investment involves trade-offs. Short-term bond funds generally invest in bonds with maturities of one to three years. Intermediate funds invest within a range of three to ten years, while long-term funds invest in maturities as long as thirty years. The following table provides an indication of the sensitivity of each type of fund to a 1% increase in the level of interest rates:

Table 4.1
BOND PRICE SENSITIVITY

Percentage change in bond price given a 1% increase in interest rates

Short-term Bond Fund	−1.3%
Intermediate-term Fund	−4.8%
Long-term Fund	−9.7%

This table suggests that shorter-term bond funds are appropriate for investors who expect rising interest rates, as well as for those who require access to their money in the near term. Longer-term funds make sense for investors who are saving for a retirement that is at least ten years away.

Having seen bonds characterized by issuer and maturity, you are now in a position to understand most types of bond mutual funds. For example, a **short-term government bond fund** invests in U.S. Government securities with maturities of one to three years. Such a fund is immune to default and will not change significantly in price as a result of a shift in interest rates. At the other extreme, a **junk bond fund** may invest in longer-term corporate bonds that are subject to default and to large swings in price. Obviously, these two funds are very different in nature, and you would certainly expect to earn a much higher return on the junk fund over time. The differences in these funds highlight an important rule: you should never purchase a bond fund strictly on the basis of its stated or advertised yield or interest rate. Funds that offer unusually high interest rates carry other kinds of risks that must be carefully evaluated.

Mortgage Bond Funds

Mortgage bond funds are popular among retirement investors, but they are somewhat complex and hard to classify. Briefly, a **mortgage bond** represents an interest in a pool of residential mortgages that are guaranteed by the U.S. Government. On a monthly basis, each homeowner in the pool makes a mortgage payment, which consists of both principal and interest, and these payments are "passed through" to the bondholders. Assuming no change in interest rates, the bondholder receives a steady stream of payments over thirty years. However, when interest rates fall, homeowners often pay off their existing mortgage by taking out a new loan at a lower rate. When a homeowner in the pool refinances, each bondholder receives his share of the principal repayment. Therefore, while a mortgage bond has a maturity of thirty years, the bondholder may actually find that most of his capital is returned following a decline in rates. On the other hand, very few people refinance during a period of rising interest rates and the bondholder recovers his principal very slowly.

The bottom line is that the maturity of a mortgage fund is relatively uncertain. The maturity gets shorter as interest rates fall and mortgages are refinanced, while it lengthens during periods of rising rates. In order to compensate the bondholder for this uncertainty, mortgage bond funds pay a higher interest rate than other high-quality alternatives. Mortgage funds do particularly well during a period of stable interest rates but perform poorly when rates move significantly in either direction.

STABLE VALUE AND MONEY MARKET FUNDS

The previous section indicated that there are several types of bond funds that do not fluctuate in price. An investor in one of these funds never realizes a gain or loss and her return is equal to the interest paid by the fund. Since these types of funds represent the most widely used option in 401(k) plans, they should be reviewed in some detail.

The simplest and most straightforward of all bond funds are **money market mutual funds,** which invest in very short-term bonds known as money market securities. Corporations, banks, and the U.S. Government issue money market securities to meet very short-term capital needs. In the case of Uncle Sam, these short-term securities are called Treasury bills. Among the short-term securities issued by corporations and banks are commercial paper, banker's acceptances, negotiable certificates of deposit, and so on.

By definition, money market securities cannot mature beyond one year, and most are actively traded and highly liquid. Additionally, most money market securities are issued by companies that are very strong financially. A money market mutual fund typically invests in securities with a maturity of approximately sixty days. Given their short maturities, the prices of these securities do not fluctuate, which renders a money market mutual fund immune to changes in interest rates. For that reason, the price of a money market fund is fixed at $1.00 per share, and investors are given the opportunity to enter or exit the fund daily. The interest rate on a money market fund changes daily, with changes in the rates paid on money market securities.

Money market funds perform well during periods of rapidly rising interest rates, because the price stays constant while the interest paid increases. In contrast, bond funds generally perform poorly in such an environment. Finally, money market funds are appropriate for investors with very short-time horizons who cannot tolerate any risk of losing principal. However, this safety has a cost. A reasonable proxy for the return on money market funds is the Treasury bill rate, which has averaged 3.7% since 1926. Remember, longer-term bonds earned an average return of 5.7% during this period.

For investors interested in stability who do not need instant access to their money, a **stable value** or **guaranteed fund** may be a better alternative to money market funds. The price of a stable value fund remains fixed, as was the case with a money market fund. However, an investor is not allowed to exit daily. Instead, access is available monthly, semiannually, or annually depending upon the fund. The return on a stable value fund generally falls between money market and bond returns. Funds with frequent openings generally provide returns that barely exceed money market rates, while those with annual access should be closer to bond returns. A fixed annuity is a form of stable value fund in that the insurance company offers a guaranteed rate of return. However, fixed annuities are designed for long-term investors, because most have very strict limitations on the withdrawal of funds.

A red flag is important here! Whereas money market funds invest in short-term, high-quality securities, a stable value fund is free to invest in a broader range of instruments. Some of these investments could fall in price in a poor market, which in turn would cause the value of the fund to decline. In order to honor the guaranteed price, the fund sponsor would have to make up the difference. Therefore, the "guarantee" in a stable value fund is only as good as the financial strength of the sponsor, which is usually a bank, insurance company, or mutual fund organization. If you decide to invest in a stable value fund or fixed annuity, ask your employer for information on the financial strength of the fund's sponsor.

Bonds Revisited

Earlier, it was seen that the best way to invest in stocks is to combine several different mutual funds that invest in a variety of domestic and foreign securities. How about bonds?

Since all bonds respond to changes in interest rates to a greater or lesser extent, combining a series of bond funds is not all that helpful. Therefore, one or two funds should meet your needs. Which types should you pick?

If you have a long time horizon and are willing to tolerate some ups and downs, a long-term government fund is probably your best bet. Corporate bonds do pay a slightly higher interest rate, but the spread is generally insufficient to take on the default risk. Investors nearing retirement are usually interested in a more conservative approach to investing, so short-term and stable value funds are right for them. Many younger investors also choose stable value funds, because they are deathly afraid of losing money. While their fears are understandable, they are giving up a significant amount of return in exchange for a level of comfort that may not be necessary.

Finally, what about junk bond funds and foreign bond funds? Of course, there is no harm in making a small allocation to either of them. However, it seems preferable to take risk in the stock market, in which returns are potentially unlimited, than to buy junk bonds, which are also risky yet carry a return that exceeds Treasury rates by only 3% or 4%. Interest rates are frequently higher in other countries, which makes foreign bonds superficially attractive. However, the interest rate advantage is generally lost through changes in the currency. The bottom line is keep it simple!

BRINGING ORDER TO CHAOS

While you may feel overwhelmed by the number of different types of mutual funds that have been described, they are all really just variations of basic stock and bond funds. One option that has not been covered is **balanced funds**. A balanced fund is a mutual fund that invests in stocks, bonds, and money market securities. Such funds are popular because they release an investor from the responsibility of deciding how much money to allocate to each of these categories at any given time. The primary drawback of balanced funds is that the investor loses the ability to determine how much risk he is willing to take. In other words, the risk of the fund is determined by its manager and not by the participant. After reading Chapter 6, you will be able to develop a blend of securities that is right for you, so a balanced fund should be unnecessary.

In order to place these broad fund categories in perspective, it might be helpful to rank them in order of risk and return. The projections included in the following table represent educated guesses as to the rates of return that an investor might expect over a long period of time. These projections are based on historical returns, with minor adjustments for recent changes in the structure of the capital markets. However, they do not take into account the current level of any market or attempt to forecast actual returns over the near term. Remember, the categories with the highest expected returns also entail the greatest risk.

Table 4.2

POPULAR RETIREMENT PLAN OPTIONS RANKED BY RISK/RETURN

Category	Projected Return
Foreign Stocks	12.0%
Small Capitalization U.S. Stocks	12.0%
Large Capitalization U.S. Stocks	10.5%
Balanced Funds	9.5%
Bond Funds	7.0%
Stable Value Funds	6.0%
Money Market Funds	5.0%

You now have a basic level of knowledge of a broad range of securities, which should allow you to read the descriptive material on a mutual fund and understand the strategy that is being employed. While your plan may offer a variety of unfamiliar options, you will find that they probably represent a variation of one of the basic categories listed in Table 4.2.

As a general rule, you should avoid funds that employ esoteric or complex strategies. Instead, by combining several of the "meat-and-potatoes" funds discussed above, you will enjoy a sophisticated investment program.

WARNING! WARNING!

Chapter 3 extolled the virtue of saving and encouraged you to participate in your employer's retirement plan. However, there is one situation in which you should be fairly cautious.

Specifically, you should be wary of any plan in which employees are not given the ability to choose among investment options. Many employers have done a very good job of making investments on behalf of their employees, but others have made poor decisions or engaged in fraudulent activity. In one case, a large retailer invested employee funds in its own stores, which became virtually worthless when the company went bankrupt. In other cases, employers have invested in art, coins, and other types of investments that are illiquid and difficult to value. Some retirement plans invest a portion of their funds in the company's own stock. This represents a "double bet" on the company, because each employee becomes dependent on the company for both current income and retirement security. Once you understand this double bet, you can make an informed decision as to whether you want to invest in company stock. But you should be very careful if this decision is forced on you by the company.

In conclusion, ask a number of hard questions before you decide to participate if your plan does not allow you to select among fairly conventional investments.

RISK

Up to this point, the word *risk* has been used many times without actually being defined. In fact, most investors have a difficult time understanding risk even though they know that they don't want very much of it. The next chapter will cover risk and the various means of controlling it. Most important, you will decide how much risk is appropriate for you.

Key Points to Remember

- Most mutual funds represent variations on basic stock and bond funds.

- The best relationship between risk and return will be achieved by combining several different types of funds in your retirement plan.

- You should be wary of plans in which you are not allowed to select from fairly conventional options.

CHAPTER 5

Investment Risk

I shall not attempt to further define hard-core pornography. But, I know it when I see it.

—Supreme Court Justice
Potter Stewart

Just as Judge Stewart had a difficult time defining smut, you are probably hard pressed to explain risk in a few sentences even though you know it when you see it.

Risk is a difficult topic for several reasons. First, the most widely used definition of risk involves some mathematics and statistics that are understandably threatening and unfamiliar to most people. Second, risk is a very personal thing, and two people with identical financial circumstances might choose very different levels of risk because of their psychological makeup. Finally, risk can be a touchy subject because it involves a great deal of emotion and, consequently, frequently causes otherwise sensible individuals to act irrationally.

Most people overestimate the risk in investing, and this misperception causes them to invest too cautiously. After all, markets *do* go up on average, and while negative years occur regularly, it is rare for a diversified portfolio to suffer a severe decline over a long period of time.

WHY IS RISK IMPORTANT?

Deep in his heart, every investor has the same objective: to earn a very high rate of return with no risk. Intellectually, we know that the world can't be that simple, but each of us harbors the secret hope that there are a few exceptions to the rule and that we will find them. Unfortunately, the real world provides a very simple and clear relationship between risk and return.

The Relationship Between Risk and Return

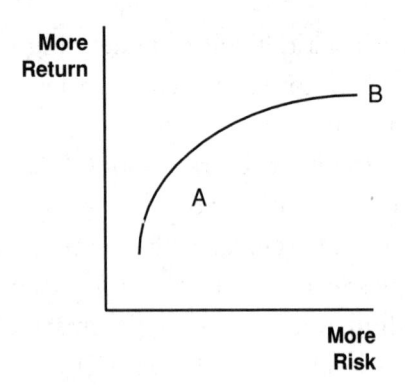

Chart 5.1

The curved line in Chart 5.1 depicts the balance between risk and reward, and each point illustrates the relationship for a particular investment. For example, investment B might represent stocks. As you will note, B is expected to generate a high rate of return. However, that return comes at a much higher level of risk than A, which represents government bonds.

The relationship between risk and return is logical and has been confirmed by dozens of careful studies. A high-risk investment that has worked out will seem to have involved very little risk, but that is after the fact! Before the fact, you should expect the inherent relationship to hold, which suggests that a high-risk investment is likely to produce a wild ride.

When given a choice, most people understandably opt for a low-to-moderate level of risk. However, as the above chart demonstrates, this decision condemns them to a low-to-moderate rate of return, which makes it more difficult to accomplish their retirement objectives. That is why risk is so important!

Of course, some people truly cannot tolerate risk, and they must be content to accept a low rate of return. But the key is to understand the true nature of risk and to strike the best balance given your personal situation and emotional makeup. Now that you know why risk is so important, we will take on the difficult task of defining it.

THE RISK OF LOSING MONEY

Most people define risk as the chance of losing money on an investment. Later, it will be suggested why this is a poor way of thinking about risk. But, since the fear of losing money is so ingrained in the minds of investors, we should carefully evaluate the behavior of different kinds of investments to see how often losses actually occur.

Table 5.1

FREQUENCY OF LOSSES (1926–1996)

Category	# of loss years	% of loss years
Large Capitalization Stocks	20	28.2
Small Capitalization Stocks	21	29.6
Foreign Stocks[*]	6	25.0
Long-term Government Bonds	19	26.8

[*] *Returns prior to 1973 for foreign stocks are not meaningful due to fixed currency exchange rates. Therefore, the table covers the period 1973–1995 for this category.*

Stable value and money market funds were excluded from the table, because they deliver positive returns every year except in the case of a significant default. Also excluded were balanced funds, since their behavior normally corresponds to a blend of stocks and bonds.

The consistency of the data in Table 5.1 is very interesting. During the past seventy-one years, most major categories of investment have suffered negative returns between 25% and 30% of the time. In other words, an investor could expect to lose money in one of every three-and-one-half years. Many people will be surprised at the frequency of losses over the 1926–1996 period, because negative returns have been fairly rare in recent years. For example, large capitalization stocks have lost money in only three of the last twenty-one years, or 14% of the time.

The more favorable experience in recent years raises the question of whether something has changed. In other words, should we expect losses to remain less frequent in the future because of some change in the financial world? Of course, no one really knows the answer. But the most prudent course is to assume that losses will continue at the more frequent rate that has prevailed since 1926. Besides, you should soon be convinced that these annual ups and downs are of little importance.

You should also note that bonds suffer losses just about as often as stocks, which seems to contradict the earlier statement that bonds offer less risk than stocks. To properly compare these categories, one must look at both the frequency of losses and the size of those losses.

Table 5.2

FREQUENCY OF SIGNIFICANT LOSSES (1926–1996)

	SMALL CAP. STOCKS	LARGE CAP. STOCKS	LONG-TERM BONDS
Annual Loss Greater than 5%	19	15	5
Annual Loss Greater than 10%	12	8	0
Annual Loss Greater than 20%	7	4	0

First, you will note that bonds suffered losses greater than 5% in only five out of the seventy-one years, or about 7% of the time. Additionally, they never fell more than 10% in any year. Combining Tables 5.1 and 5.2, you should conclude that bonds do suffer losses regularly but that they are almost always very modest in size.

What about stocks? Not only do stocks suffer losses regularly, they occasionally decline by 10%, 20%, or even more. For example, large capitalization stocks have declined by more than 20% in four out of the past seventy-one years, or 6% of the time. If the same pattern holds true in the future, then an individual who invests exclusively in stocks for her entire working career could expect to suffer a 20% decline during two or three of the forty years. Small capitalization stocks are subject to even bigger swings, as demonstrated by the fact that they have declined by more than 20% in seven of the seventy-one years, or 10% of the time.

After studying this data, you are probably tempted to avoid stocks like the plague. Yes, they *do* suffer losses regularly. However, those losses are almost temporary in nature. In order to truly understand the risk of losing money, you must evaluate the chance of a loss over a longer period of time. Stated another way, how quickly do stocks recover from losses when they occur?

Table 5.3

HISTORICAL RETURNS ON STOCKS (1901–1996)

	1-YEAR PERIOD	5-YEAR PERIODS	10-YEAR PERIODS	20-YEAR PERIODS
NUMBER OF PERIODS	96	92	87	77
Maximum Annual Return	54.0%	29.1%	19.8%	16.7%
Worst Annual Return	-43.4%	-12.5%	-.9%	3.1%
Number of Negative Returns	27	9	2	0

This table provides some fascinating information regarding the return on large capitalization stocks during this century. You will note that there have been ninety-two 5-year and eighty-seven 10-year periods during this ninety-six-year interval. How can that be?

This table measures rolling periods, which means that 1901–1905 is counted as the first 5-year period, 1902–1906 represents the second, and so on. In other words, these periods overlap. This method of analyzing data is useful because it provides more data points than would be available from consecutive periods.

What can we learn from this table? First, it confirms the previous statement that stocks prices vary significantly from year to year. As was mentioned earlier, annual stock returns ranged between 54% and negative 43%, and negative returns were realized in twenty-seven of the ninety-six years. However, notice what happens as the time frame is increased. Over 5-year periods, the range of annual returns narrows considerably and the number of negative periods decreases from 27 to nine. Only two 10-year periods have recorded negative returns, and the worst of them was very modest at -.9%. Most important, investors have never lost money in a 20-year period. The bottom line is that stocks do suffer from regular losses, but those declines are almost always followed by recoveries such that it is very rare to lose money for periods of five years or longer. In fact, the losses experienced during even the worst bear markets are typically recouped within a period of three to four years.

The Impact of Time

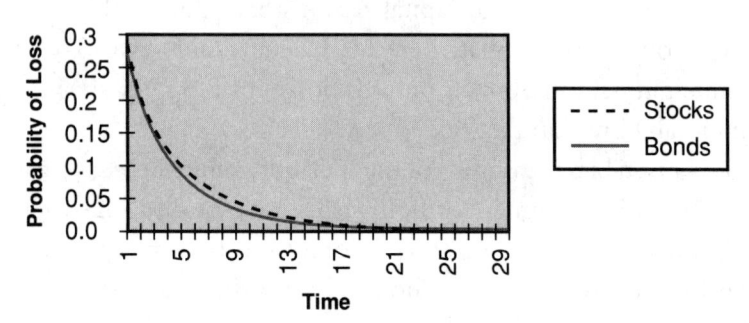

Chart 5.2

Chart 5.2 provides a graphic representation of the data included in Table 5.3. As you will note, stocks have between a 25% and 30% chance of losing money in any given year. But the probability of losing money decreases rapidly as the time horizon is lengthened, and the odds approach zero after about fifteen years. The pattern is similar for bonds and other types of securities, although the odds of losing money are slightly lower across all time periods.

TIME

Hopefully, you have picked up on one of the most important concepts in financial planning, which is that the length of an investor's time horizon has a major influence on the way he should invest his money. For example, stocks represent a risky investment for someone who plans to spend his capital in one year's time, because the return during that year could range between 54% and negative 43%. In other words, there is great uncertainty as to the value of his investment at the end of one year. On the other hand, stocks seem very appropriate for an investor who is twenty years away from retirement. She can expect to earn a higher rate of return than would be available from bonds or stable value funds, and she has plenty of time to recover from a downdraft in the stock market. The impact of time will be considered in more detail when the factors that you should evaluate when selecting an appropriate level of risk for your retirement fund are discussed.

ARE YOU KIDDING ME?

Having read the last couple of sections, you are probably very skeptical. After all, they seem to be saying that losses do not matter. In fact, *temporary* losses *don't* matter. A temporary loss is simply a short-term decline in value, which is likely to be recovered over a reasonable period assuming the investor sits tight. But *permanent* losses are declines in value that cannot be recovered, and they matter a lot.

What are some examples of permanent losses? First, a permanent loss occurs when a significant amount of money is committed to a single investment that goes bad. For instance, suppose you purchase a junk bond and the issuer is subsequently forced into bankruptcy because of a downturn in the economy. Assuming the company never recovers, your investment will be wiped out, and there is no way to recover this loss. This form of permanent loss is easily avoidable by investing in a diversified portfolio of stocks and high-quality bonds.

A permanent loss can also occur if you "sell at the bottom." Suppose you panic and sell all of your stocks following a sharp decline in the market. As a result of the market trauma, you will likely invest the proceeds of the sale in a low-risk vehicle such as a money market fund. While the stock market will bounce back, you will not, because you have chosen a "safe" investment that will produce a low rate of return. Even if you ultimately recover your original capital, you will never get back onto the trajectory that was assumed in your retirement plan. Obviously, this type of loss can be avoided by riding out the ups and downs in the stock market without overreacting.

Finally, a permanent loss occurs when the market drops at the wrong time. For example, let's assume that you were planning to purchase a fixed annuity at retirement. Further, assume that all of your retirement assets are invested in stocks and the stock market falls 25% immediately prior to your retirement date. As a result of the crash, your accumulated assets will decrease by 25%, which means that your annuity will produce 25% less income than expected. At that point, your only choices are to accept the lower level of income or to continue working until the market recovers. This type of loss is generally avoidable by switching your retirement fund into more stable investments as you approach your planned retirement date.

In summary, the risk of losing money is very low for long-term investors who stick to their program and plan their investments intelligently. Besides, as was mentioned earlier, the chance of losing money is not a very good measure of risk. Why not? A simple example will make the point.

Based on standard tables that assume a return of 8%, you have decided to save 10% of your salary every year for retirement. Since you are deathly afraid of losing any of your hard-earned money, you invest your funds in a stable value account that earns an average return of 6% over the course of your career. By definition, stable value funds never suffer a loss, so you have been able to sail through your career without taking any risk. Wait a minute! Because you earned a return of 6% as compared to the 8% assumption, you will come up short at retirement. In fact, you are going to have 27% less income than projected! That sounds like risk to me. In other words, the risk of loss is an inadequate measure because it does not take into account an individual's investment objective. The risk of loss does not take into account the likelihood that an investor will reach his goal.

Isn't the true measure of risk the chance that you will not reach your retirement objective? This idea will be discussed in more detail later in this chapter. Having beaten the risk of loss to death, let's move on to another popular way of measuring risk.

VOLATILITY

The measure of risk that is used by most academics and practitioners today is the **volatility** of return. Virtually every financial publication includes graphics similar to Chart 4.1 (page 58), in which two or more investments are compared on a grid that measures risk and return. The risk measure that is used in these charts is the standard deviation of return, which is a measure of volatility. Standard deviation is defined as the amount by which the return on a given investment fluctuates around its average return. Here is a simple example to clarify this murky concept. Over a five-year period, two investments earn the following annual rates of return:

	INVESTMENT A	INVESTMENT B
Year 1	8%	12%
Year 2	8%	-15%
Year 3	8%	20%
Year 4	8%	5%
Year 5	8%	22.5%

At the end of five years both investments will be worth the same amount of money, because they earned the same average rate of return. But which investment would allow you to sleep better at night? Obviously, the return on B is quite volatile, because it fluctuates considerably from year to year.

Why does volatility represent risk? Continuing with this example, suppose you thought that there was a chance that you might have to liquidate your investment sometime during the next five years. In the case of Investment A, you could forecast the amount of proceeds that you would receive from the sale with some confidence, because its return is so stable. On the other hand, you would be hard pressed to guess the value of B at any given future date.

Simply stated, volatility creates uncertainty as to the potential value of an investment, and investors dislike uncertainty intensely. One of the subtleties of this measure of risk is that volatility can occur in either direction. While the word *risk* has a purely negative connotation, volatility or risk is welcomed by investors as long as the fluctuations are in the right direction.

Why is volatility the preferred measure of risk? First, standard deviation is a simple statistic that is easy to calculate, and it allows the risk of every type of investment to be compared on an apples-to-apples basis. More important, there are actually many different kinds of risk that could affect a given investment. Investors face credit risk, inflation risk, interest rate risk, market risk, prepayment risk, and so on. The beauty of the volatility of return is that it encompasses all of them. When analyzing a given security, an investor considers each of these risks and then makes a decision to buy or sell. Other investors do the same thing and their collective decisions cause the price of the security to rise and fall, which represents volatility. Stated another way, volatility takes into account everything that market participants know about a given security and its risks. If there is considerable uncertainty regarding the prospects for a security, its price will gyrate as market participants buy and sell.

Since an investor is concerned about future volatility, how do practitioners forecast standard deviation? In general, they measure historical standard deviation for a security or market and then project the historical data into the future. Given a series of monthly or annual returns, standard deviation can be calculated using the statistical function that is built into most hand calculators. Because markets do change, some investors weigh the recent past more heavily when calculating historical data. Others adjust the data for a "fudge factor" to take into account perceived changes in the investment climate.

While the standard deviation of return is widely used, this measure of risk has two drawbacks. First, volatility can change over time. For example, U.S. stocks have been about one-third less volatile during the last few years than their long-term average. Does this mean that something has changed fundamentally such that we should expect a permanent decrease in volatility, or have we been in an unusually calm period that is not likely to be repeated soon? This is much more than an academic question. If the volatility of stocks really has declined without a commensurate decrease in return, then most investors should raise their exposure to stocks. On the other hand, if investors have become overly comfortable with stocks because of the low level of volatility, they are in for a rude awakening if fluctuations return to the historical norm.

UNDERSTANDING VOLATILITY

The real problem with standard deviation as a measure of risk is that most people do not know enough about statistics to interpret it. For example, suppose that you visit the Benefits department of your employer in order to make some decisions regarding the investments that you will include in your 401(k) plan. Typically, you will be supplied with brochures prepared by several different mutual fund and insurance companies. Inevitably, these brochures include a risk/return graph showing that stocks have experienced more volatility than bonds. For example, the chart might indicate a standard deviation of 18% for stocks and 11% for bonds. While you understand from these statistics that stocks are more volatile, what does this mean for you? Can you live with a standard deviation of 18%, or is 11% more appropriate? By the way, what does a standard deviation of 18% really mean?

You undoubtedly are not interested in a lecture on statistics, but a little knowledge will help you understand some risk measures that will be included in several tables in the next chapter. Stock and bond returns behave according to the normal probability distribution that is better known as the bell-shaped curve.

The Bell-Shaped Curve

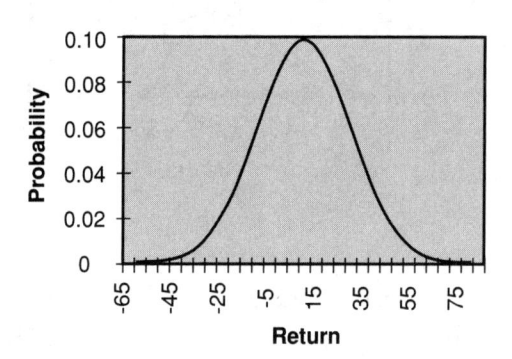

Chart 5.3

Chart 5.3 illustrates the bell-shaped curve for an investment that is expected to provide an average return of 11%. The horizontal axis depicts a range of possible returns, and the vertical axis indicates the probability or chance that each return will be realized in a given year. For the purposes of this example, the scale is of no importance, so you should focus strictly on the shape of the curve. The highest point, or peak, of the curve represents the average return of 11%, since it is the most likely outcome. As you will note, returns on either side of the average are also very likely, but the probabilities begin to fall dramatically as you move away from the average. While much higher or lower returns are possible, they are much less likely, as depicted by the "tails" on each end of the bell.

Standard Deviation

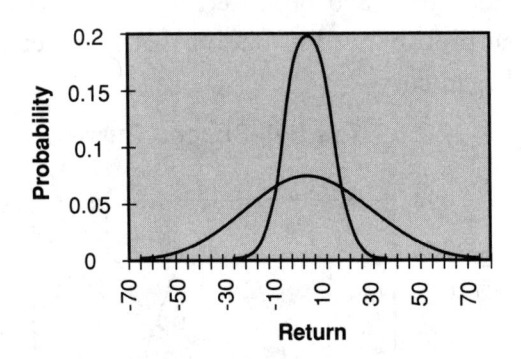

[Chart showing two bell-shaped curves with Probability (0 to 0.2) on y-axis and Return (-70 to 70) on x-axis]

Chart 5.4

Chart 5.4 illustrates the bell-shaped curve for two different investments. In one case, the returns fall within a narrow band, which means that it should experience low volatility. In contrast, the more volatile investment is characterized by a curve with wide tails, because extreme returns become more likely. The width of the bell is measured by standard deviation.

Only two forecasts are required to draw the bell-shaped curve: the expected return and the standard deviation of return. Once we know what the curve looks like, we can estimate the odds that certain events will occur. For example, suppose stocks earn an average return of 11% with a standard deviation of 18%. In fact, these statistics are very close to the historic averages. By crunching some numbers and referring to a normal probability table, we can make some very useful statements about the likely behavior of stocks in the future. For example, we can estimate that stocks will lose money about 28% of the time, or in one of every three-and-one-half years. Similarly, we can calculate the chance that stocks will lose 10% or 20% in a given year. On the other side of the coin, we find that stocks will earn a return greater than 10% in fifty-two out of one hundred years. This suggests that an individual with a 10% return objective has a better-than-even chance of accomplishing her goal. The bottom line is that the standard deviation or volatility of an investment does not tell you very much by itself. However, when combined with the expected rate of return, it provides a great deal of useful information.

Where is all of this headed? Just as it is easy to draw the bell-shaped curve for stocks, we can follow the same steps to draw the curve for a combination of U.S. stocks, foreign stocks, bonds, and so on. In other words, we can estimate the future behavior for any portfolio. Of course, our predictions are subject to error, but this type of analysis will give you confidence in the strategy that you choose because you will have a good sense of where your retirement fund is headed and what might happen to it in any given year. When a bad year actually occurs, you won't be surprised, and you will be less likely to make an emotional and damaging decision to sell at the bottom.

THE RISK OF COMING UP SHORT

While most people worry about losing money on their investments, this is not a serious issue in most cases. However, most participants in retirement plans should be worried about the risk of coming up short. In other words, because they are too cautious in the way they invest their funds, they are likely to earn a return that is not sufficient to meet their retirement income objectives.

The following chart indicates the probability that stocks and bonds will earn a 9% return for various time frames. As you will note, stocks offer pretty good odds over the short term, but the probability increases with time. In contrast, bonds offer a lower probability of earning 9%, and the picture gets worse with time. Simply stated, lower-risk investments increase the chance of coming up short.

Shortfall Risk

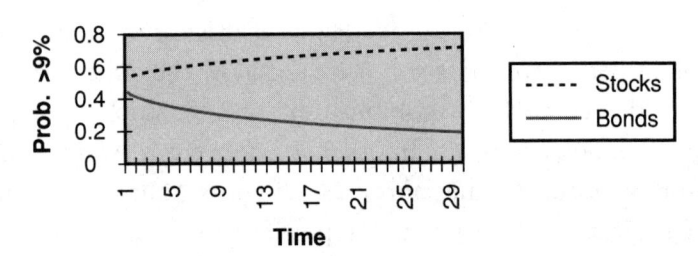

Chart 5.5

To make this point more personal, why don't we consider a "typical" employee. We will assume that this individual joins the company at age twenty-five but does not participate in the retirement plan until age thirty because of the cost of establishing his household. From that point forward, he contributes 5% of salary to the plan every year, which is matched by 5% from the company. (In fact, such a match is more generous than the typical plan.) Table 4.2 (page 67) provided some educated guesses as to future rates of return on various types of investments. As you may recall, returns of 5% to 7% were forecast on low-risk categories such as money market, stable value, and bond funds. Let's assume that this individual is very concerned about losing any money, which leads him to invest in a stable value fund that earns

6%. At retirement, he will have accumulated only enough assets to provide a replacement ratio of 30%. If Social Security continues to exist in its current form, he may get to a total replacement ratio of 60% or 70%. In other words, the best case results in a level of income that is barely acceptable, and the worst case is a disaster. On the other hand, suppose he had invested in a reasonable blend of stocks and bonds that generated a return of 9.75%. In this case, his fund would replace 55% of salary, which results in a replacement ratio of 85% assuming the expected contribution from Social Security.

The bottom line is that retirement savers are much more exposed to the risk of a mediocre return than to losing money. While a short-term decline in the market is of little consequence, a poor return over the long haul will result in irreversible damage.

RISK IN PERSPECTIVE

Having considered investment risk from several perspectives, we are now ready to tie it all together. Ideally, you would like to minimize both the volatility of your investments and the chance of coming up short. Unfortunately, you will be unable to eliminate both risks, so the trick is to come up with the right compromise. The ideal balance would provide you with a return that is sufficient to accomplish your retirement goals while also limiting volatility to an acceptable level. In other words, your investments must deliver your target rate of return without subjecting you to a short-term decline in value that would unnerve you.

The following example makes this point more forcefully. Consider two investments that offer projected returns of 11% and 7%, respectively. Since there is no such thing as a free lunch, the first investment is more volatile, as measured by a standard deviation of 18% compared to 11% for the other alternative. For an investor who is seeking a 9% return, the first investment offers better than a 60% chance of achieving the target over five years, whereas the odds are only 35% for the lower-returning alternative. However, the first alternative is twice as likely to suffer a 10% annual loss, and it will occasionally get clobbered. In contrast, the second investment is essentially immune to large losses.

In case you haven't solved the riddle, these two investments represent stocks and bonds, and the solution lies in combining them in the correct proportion. The next chapter recommends several portfolios that involve different blends of securities. Using the bell-shaped curve for each portfolio, it provides information on the potential for losses of various sizes as well as the odds of coming up short. You will be pleasantly surprised that these portfolios offer attractive returns and relative stability.

HOW DO YOU CONTROL RISK?

Now that you know what risk is, the next question is how to control it. There are two principal means of managing risk: **diversification** and **asset allocation**.

DIVERSIFICATION

Diversification is the process of including a number of different types of securities in a portfolio. It is an effort to reduce the impact of any individual investment. Diversification eliminates the chance of becoming fabulously wealthy by putting all of your money into one investment that soars in value. On the other hand, it also prevents you from being wiped out by a loser.

Why does diversification reduce risk? As was mentioned earlier, the prices of different securities do not always move in tandem in the marketplace. In a diversified portfolio, some securities will inevitably decline in value during any particular time period. However, others will enjoy price increases at the same time, which smooths out the violent ups and downs.

The key to constructing a relatively stable portfolio is to combine investments that do not move together. A statistic known as the correlation coefficient measures the extent to which two investments move in tandem. A correlation of 1 means that the investments move in lock-step, while a coefficient of -1 indicates that they move in the opposite direction. A coefficient that is close to zero suggests that their movements are unrelated. The objective is to combine investments with correlations that are close to zero, or perhaps even negative. In fact, the ideal portfolio would consist of two investments that generally increase in value over time but move in the opposite direction over short periods (a correlation of -1). A blend of these two investments would increase in value in a straight line, because their ups and downs would exactly cancel each other out.

In the real world, it is fairly difficult to find two investments that have negative correlation. Instead, most types of securities move in the same direction, although the relationship between their movements may be fairly weak. For example, the correlation between U.S. stocks and bonds has been about .3 during the past ten years. But as long as two investments do not move exactly in tandem, combining them will improve diversification. In fact, as demonstrated in Chart 5.6, the diversification provided by a blend of fairly conventional securities results in an attractive balance between risk and return.

The Power of Diversification

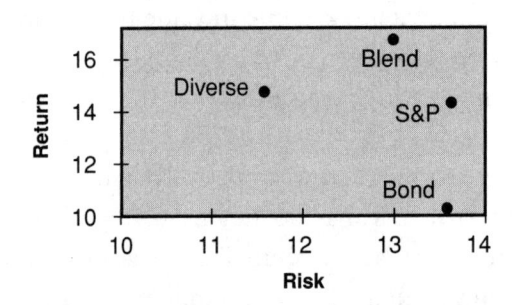

[Chart showing Return vs. Risk with four points: Blend (~13.5 risk, ~16.5 return), Diverse (~11.5 risk, ~15 return), S&P (~13.5 risk, ~14 return), Bond (~13.5 risk, ~10 return)]

Chart 5.6

Chart 4.1 (page 58) displayed the risk/return trade-off for the S&P 500 and a blend of large capitalization, small capitalization, and foreign stocks. As you will recall, the blended portfolio provided both a higher rate of return and a lower level of risk. Chart 5.6, above, has the addition of two points: the first represents bonds and the second, a diverse blend of bonds and several different categories of stocks. Note that the "Diverse" portfolio has generated a return that is only modestly below that of the blend of stocks with considerably less risk. In other words, adding bonds to a stock portfolio significantly reduces risk without a commensurate decrease in return. More important, the diverse portfolio actually entailed less risk than bonds with a considerable increase in return. As was discussed in Chapter 4, many participants in retirement plans place all of their money in bond or stable value funds because they are considered safe. Chart 5.6 indicates that a diversified portfolio of different types of stocks and bonds is also relatively safe yet provides a superior rate of return.

Portfolios should be diversified at two levels. First, most portfolios should contain several different types or classes of investments. The "Diverse" portfolio in Chart 5.6 consisted of bonds and three different types of stocks. Second, each category should contain a large number of individual securities. For example, a stock portfolio requires at least twenty individual holdings to achieve a reasonable level of diversification. In fact, a larger number is preferable unless the twenty are very carefully selected to ensure that they represent a broad range of industries. Most stock mutual funds hold a minimum of fifty securities, and some hold as many as one thousand. For that reason, individual security diversification should not represent a problem for retirement savers who invest in mutual funds. However, there are two exceptions that should be noted. First, a fixed annuity or stable value fund represents an obligation of one company regardless of the level of diversification that the company achieves in its underlying portfolio. Therefore, you should exercise a good deal of caution in selecting these products. Second, the decision to concentrate your retirement fund in your company's own stock results in a very undiversified portfolio. While you may hit a home run, it is a very risky approach that you should not undertake lightly.

In summary, diversification is an essential means of protecting your retirement fund from a financial disaster. If you learn nothing from this book other than the importance of diversification, it will have served you well. Diversification does not allow you to fine-tune the level of risk in your portfolio; it simply is a means of minimizing unnecessary risk. In contrast, asset allocation is a tool that can be used to select the best blend of risk and return to meet your needs.

Asset Allocation

Asset allocation is the process of dividing your money among the different types of investments that are available through your retirement plan. Should you allocate 70% of your funds to stocks, or is a 30% weighting more appropriate? Should you invest in bond mutual funds or in low-risk money market funds? The asset allocation decision is critical because it will largely determine the return that you earn and the amount of risk that you take. A number of careful studies have shown that more than 90% of return is attributable to asset allocation, while individual security selection and market timing account for less than 10%. The great irony is that most media attention is focused on the two factors that account for less than 10% of return. Hardly a day passes without a newspaper article that evaluates the outlook for the stock market, and experts regularly offer their hot stock picks on investment-oriented radio shows. In contrast, asset allocation does not get very much air time, which means that most investors make this critical decision in an uninformed way.

Why does the asset mix determine the risk and return on a portfolio? The return on any given stock or bond mutual fund is largely driven by the return on the stock or bond market. When stocks are rising, most stocks tend to rise to a greater or lesser extent and bonds respond in a similar way to changes in interest rates. Of course, you hope the fund that you choose will do a little bit better than average, but that advantage is likely to be small in comparison to the impact of the overall market. Since the return on any given stock or bond fund is determined largely by the market, the return on your portfolio will be determined by the percentage you allocate to each market and not by the vehicles you choose.

How do you change the risk and return on your portfolio by varying the asset mix? If you are interested in a higher-risk portfolio, you simply emphasize higher-risk asset categories such as small capitalization stocks. In order to dampen risk, you emphasize bond, stable value, and money market funds. In the previous two sentences, the word *emphasize* was chosen carefully to remind you of the importance of diversification. Rather than making all-or-nothing decisions, you should make sure your portfolio contains between three and five different investment categories with weightings that vary according to your objectives. Table 5.4 illustrates a simple example of the power of asset allocation.

Table 5.4
THE ASSET ALLOCATION DECISION (1901–1996)

	75% STOCKS/ 25% BONDS	25% STOCKS/ 75% BONDS
Average Annual Return	9.2%	6.9%
Number of Loss Years	25	19
Years with Losses Greater than 10%	9	1
Years with Losses Greater than 20%	4	0
Worst Annual Loss	-32.9%	-12.2%

This table compares the actual returns on a portfolio consisting of 75% stocks and 25% bonds, with an alternative in which the weightings were reversed. As you would expect, the portfolio with significant exposure to stocks provided a higher rate of return, at 9.2%, as compared to 6.9% for the more conservative alternative. Over the course of a career, a difference in return of this magnitude will have a huge impact on terminal wealth. On the other hand, the first alternative was subject to frequent annual losses, and it suffered a 32.9% decline in 1931. In contrast, the worst-case loss on the second alternative was limited to 12.2%. Obviously, these two portfolios have very different risk/return characteristics despite the fact that they were invested in the same securities. The bottom line is that it is possible to structure an array of portfolios to meet the needs of different individuals by varying the weightings in several asset categories.

You are now familiar with the concept of investment risk and have at least a general knowledge of the tools that are available to control it. The next chapter will provide detailed information on the risk associated with various recommended portfolio structures. In order to select one of those alternatives, you must first decide how much risk you are willing and able to take.

THE LIFE CYCLE APPROACH TO RISK

While each person's situation is unique, most of us follow a fairly predictable path through our lives that is known as the financial life cycle. Various financial planners apply different labels to the various stages in the life cycle. Moreover, the age at which each stage begins and ends varies from one person to the next. But the basic concept is logical and widely accepted. In this version, each individual passes through four stages during her adult life. Most important, a different level of investment risk is generally appropriate at each stage.

The first is known as the household formation stage, and it begins at the time an individual becomes employed and lasts through age thirty or so. During this period, most individuals have only a modest level of income, and some are burdened by loans that were used to fund education. Additionally, most people enter this period with relatively few worldly goods, which means that any extra income is likely to be put aside to acquire and furnish a home. For all of these reasons, few people in this stage are able to make a substantial commitment to retirement saving. However, any money that is allocated to a retirement plan can be invested very aggressively. After all, this money may be invested for forty years or more, and any savings is likely to be small in comparison to the individual's future earning power. For this person, a temporary downturn in the market is truly meaningless, which means that a high level of volatility is acceptable.

Table 5.5
THE LIFE CYCLE APPROACH TO RISK

STAGE	TYPICAL RISK LEVEL
Household Formation	High
Early Accumulation	Moderate to High
Maximum Accumulation	Moderate
Retirement	Low to Moderate

The second era is known as the early accumulation stage, and it spans the period from age thirty to about fifty. During this period, most people have the ability to allocate more of their income to savings, because they have enjoyed salary growth and have completed the process of establishing their household. In other words, they should have some discretionary income. An aggressive investment strategy continues to make sense during this stage, since retirement lies fifteen to thirty years in the future. Remember, stocks have never lost money during a twenty-year period. However, most people become more cautious with age, which means that it is perfectly reasonable for an individual to tone down the level of risk in her retirement fund by a notch or two.

Stage three is a time for maximum accumulation, and it encompasses the period from age fifty right up to the point of retirement. At this point, many people will have paid off the mortgage on their home, and the kids should be out of the nest and off the family payroll. Moreover, an individual is likely to be at the pinnacle of her career, which implies a peak level of earnings. All of these factors should allow for a high level of savings. Most people begin to tone down the risk in their retirement fund during this stage by increasing their weighting in bonds, stable value funds, and the like. In some cases, this change in strategy is a function of the increasing conservatism that naturally comes with age. However, for those individuals who plan to purchase a fixed annuity at retirement, capital preservation becomes an overriding concern.

The last stage covers the retirement years themselves. Conventional wisdom suggests that retirees should focus their investment strategy on capital preservation and income generation. In other words, they should invest very conservatively. As is often the case, the conventional wisdom is only partially correct. Clearly, most retirees have no business investing in highly speculative securities. However, they do need to protect themselves against a decline in their living standard due to the effects of inflation. This goal can be accomplished by maintaining an allocation to stocks, which should generate high returns and increasing income.

In summary, the financial life cycle implies that most investors should start out with an aggressive investment program that entails a high level of risk. As time passes, they should slowly decrease the level of risk in their retirement fund, although it is important to maintain at least some exposure to growth-oriented investments during retirement. In Chapter 6, four different asset mixes are recommended, and each one is appropriate for one of the four stages in the investor life cycle. Portfolio One is reasonably aggressive and is designed for the first stage. Portfolios Two through Four entail decreasing levels of risk, and they correspond to the remaining periods.

After reviewing the information on each portfolio, someone could easily conclude that she is not comfortable with the level of risk recommended for her stage in life. For example, a younger investor might decide that Portfolio One is too volatile. At the other extreme, a retired individual might decide that he wants to speculate with a portion of his funds. What should they do? These portfolios are designed for the average investor, and it is perfectly reasonable for any given person to stray from the norm. The younger investor will accomplish her objectives by moving down the risk scale to Portfolio Two or Three, while the retiree may also want to move to Portfolio Two or Three from the recommended level of Four.

Suppose you are uncomfortable with the recommended level of risk but are having a hard time deciding where you fit. What factors should you evaluate in order to make a good decision?

PERSONALIZING RISK

Five factors should be considered when evaluating investment risk. As was suggested earlier, the most important single variable is **time**.

Time is important for two reasons. First, the odds of a poor return decrease with time, which suggests that investors with long-time horizons can afford to invest in more aggressive investments that are subject to a great deal of short-term volatility. Second, time provides an individual with the opportunity to adjust his plans in response to an unfavorable investment. For example, suppose a younger person commits to a very risky investment that results in a total loss of his capital. While such an outcome is easily preventable, it does occasionally happen. Happily, all is not lost, because this individual has plenty of time to recover. He will be forced to increase his saving rate, which may be somewhat painful, but it is very important that he not revert to highly conservative investments. But with a little discipline, there is no reason that he should not be able to accomplish his original objectives. In contrast, a severe loss that occurs within a few years of retirement can be catastrophic because there is no time to recover.

A second important variable is an individual's earning power, which economists call **human capital**. A person with a high level of income or the expectation of significant growth in income can afford to take more risk because of her ability to steer more discretionary dollars into her retirement fund should she suffer poor investment results. In contrast, people with modest incomes are generally hard pressed to find any room in their budget for retirement saving. Increasing their contribution to make up for poor returns would be unthinkable. A related issue is job security. Once again, an individual with a secure income stream can afford to take more risk, because there is little chance that she will have to tap her retirement fund to make ends meet during a period of unemployment. In contrast, potential victims of corporate downsizing will want to emphasize lower-risk, highly liquid investment alternatives.

Third, you need to think about your **financial responsibilities** and the number of dependents that you have. A single employee can afford to take considerable risk, because she need only worry about her own financial security. In contrast, a parent who is the sole provider of income to the family must be concerned about educational expenses, retirement income, medical costs, and a variety of other factors.

An individual who has **other resources** can also afford to be much more aggressive in his retirement fund because of the security that those assets provide. Examples of other resources include an inheritance, trust funds, a pension fund from a previous job, assets of a spouse, or a family business. If you enjoy any of these resources, you should consider their size in relation to your retirement fund, liquidity, the existence of any restrictions or tax issues, and so on.

The final factor is very important and rather difficult to quantify. What is your **emotional makeup**? How will you react when you learn from the evening news that the market fell dramatically? If you are the sort of person who might make rush changes in your portfolio in response to such an event, you will be better served by maintaining a lower-risk portfolio. As was mentioned earlier, emotional responses generally result in poor decisions in the investment world. On the other hand, a higher-risk portfolio will work fine if you have the ability to check on that portfolio periodically without worrying about day-to-day fluctuations. The importance of selecting a risk level that is right for your psyche can't be overestimated. While the case has been made for higher-risk portfolios, they are not right for everyone. If fluctuation in your fund will cause you anxiety, you should opt for one of the lower-risk alternatives.

RISK REDUX

This is undoubtedly more than you ever wanted to know about risk, but the success of your investment program will hinge on the way you deal with it. The portfolios recommended in Chapter 6 are quite diversified, and they were developed using the best asset allocation technology available. They provide an attractive balance between risk and return.

The decision as to which portfolio is right for you is very personal. For most people, the financial life cycle dictates the correct decision. However, if you do not feel comfortable with the portfolio recommended for your stage in life, move up or down the risk scale after considering the factors that were discussed. But don't forget that lower risk means lower returns, which will make it more difficult for you to accomplish your goals. Once again, it's your money and your life!

Key Points to Remember

- The true measure of risk is the chance of performing poorly relative to your objectives.

- The ideal portfolio is one that balances the risk of coming up short with the risk of short-term fluctuations.

- Risk is controllable through diversification and asset allocation.

- Time is the most important factor in determining how much risk you should take.

CHAPTER 6

Creating a Portfolio

Alchemy—The process of transforming something common into something special.

—WEBSTER'S COLLEGIATE DICTIONARY

During medieval times, there was widespread belief in alchemy, the magical process by which common metals supposedly were converted into gold. As noted above, a more contemporary definition refers to the conversion of anything ordinary into something special. Unfortunately, very few of us are lucky enough to witness magic, but the investment world provides one of the rare opportunities to do so.

As has been mentioned, a well-structured portfolio of investments is superior to the sum of its parts. Stated another way, a combination of plain vanilla investments can be combined into a portfolio with superior risk/return characteristics. This chapter will discuss the mechanics of building a portfolio and recommend four alternatives designed to meet the needs of investors at various stages in life. Additionally, a strategy will be suggested for moving from your current structure to the recommended portfolios. And finally, the ongoing maintenance of your investments once they are established will be considered.

THE CONCEPT OF A PORTFOLIO

Since the word *portfolio* has been mentioned many times throughout this book, it merits definition. A **portfolio** is simply a collection of securities owned by an investor. While that sounds simple enough, the examples included in Chapter 5 were designed to show you that there really *is* magic in the creation of a portfolio.

Just to refresh your memory, a blend of securities will always be less volatile than a proportionate blend of the securities' individual risks, and it is possible that a blended portfolio will have less risk than any of the securities by themselves. This property is known as diversification and results from the fact that securities do not move exactly in tandem. Second, through the magic of asset allocation, we can create a portfolio designed to produce specific levels of risk and return. While there is certainly an art to investing, these techniques illustrate the science of finance, which allows us to engineer portfolios to meet individual needs.

The most important implication of modern finance is that the risk of an investment cannot be analyzed in isolation. Instead, the key issue is the extent to which a given investment changes the overall risk of the portfolio. For example, emerging market stocks may be very volatile, but adding them to a portfolio of U.S. stocks may reduce risk because of their low correlation. What does this mean to you? First, you should spend a lot more time developing your investment objectives and asset allocation than selecting specific mutual funds. Second, you should be willing to include volatile investments in your portfolio, because they really aren't very risky when viewed in the proper context.

OPTIMAL PORTFOLIOS

Chapter 5 discussed the importance of asset allocation, the process of allocating your dollars among stocks, bonds, money market funds, and other investment options that are available through your retirement plan. In the absence of some guidance, this decision is really quite daunting.

Suppose, for example, your retirement plan offers just three investment alternatives and requires that you allocate your money among them in 5% increments. In this case, you'll have 231 different portfolios to choose from! Now, consider the increasingly common situation in which an employee has access to dozens of alternatives with no minimum investment and the ability to switch among funds daily. This employee is faced with the problem of choosing one portfolio from an infinite number of alternatives.

How in the world can anyone make this decision in a sensible manner? As it turns out, we now have the technology to analyze portfolios in a careful, organized way.

Dr. Harry Markowitz won the Nobel Prize in economics for proposing the idea of an optimal portfolio, which is defined as the portfolio that delivers the highest projected return for a given level of risk. In other words, once you select an appropriate level of risk, which combination of securities from among all of the alternatives delivers the most return? Chart 6.1 presents this idea in graphic terms.

Optimal Portfolios

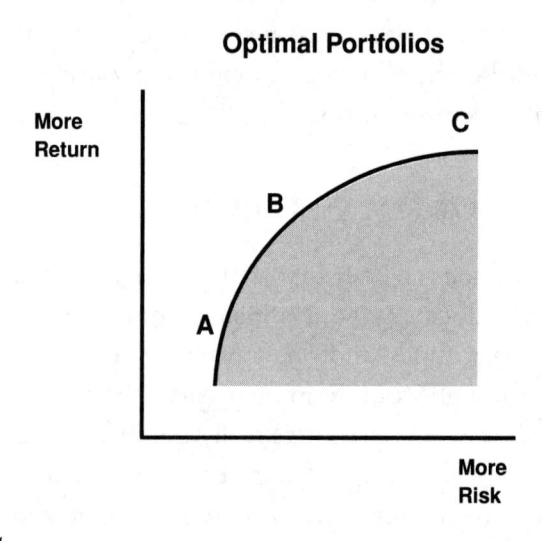

Chart 6.1

MORE RISK

You should now be familiar with this type of chart, which displays the risk and return on different types of investments. Based on forecasts of risk and return for stocks, bonds, and other types of securities, it is easy to calculate the projected risk and return on any portfolio or blend of these securities. Each of the infinite number of points in the gray area of the chart represents the risk/reward relationship for a different blend of stocks, bonds, and other assets. The optimal portfolios are those that fall along the dark line, such as A, B, or C.

In each case, no other portfolio provides a higher return for the risk involved.

The critical point is that no rational investor will hold a portfolio that does not fall on the line, because it would be inferior. While this sounds reasonable in theory, can you in fact identify these optimal portfolios? In addition to proposing the concept of optimal portfolios, Markowitz described the basic technique that could be used to identify them—a technique now incorporated in computer programs known as optimizers. Retirement plan vendors use these programs to develop the asset mixes that they recommend to participants. In fact, some vendors make available representatives who will use these tools to help you develop a custom portfolio to meet your needs. Whether you accept your vendor's standard recommendations or develop a custom asset mix, you will be more comfortable with the portfolio that you select if you have a basic understanding of the **optimization** process.

Briefly, three steps are involved. First, you must decide which types of investments to include in your portfolio. Second, the computer program requires forecasts of risk and return for each investment category. Third, you have the opportunity to constrain the program. For example, you might decide that you are uncomfortable with more than 20% exposure to non–U.S. stocks even if the computer favors a higher weighting. While a constrained portfolio may be more familiar and comfortable, this comfort can be costly, because the constraints result in a lower return for the risk assumed. After completing these steps, the computer takes over and recommends a different portfolio structure for each level of risk. Let's focus on the required inputs in a little more detail.

Investment Options

First, how many different types of investments should you include in your portfolio and which ones should you select? As was discussed in the last chapter, diversification is the most effective tool in controlling risk, which should lead you toward a larger number of categories. Large institutional investors such as pension and endowment funds frequently hold as many as ten different asset classes in their portfolios. On the other hand, a portfolio consisting of a large number of mutual funds may become unmanageable for an individual, and the added diversification becomes minimal at some point. These latter points favor a smaller number of categories.

Once again, the name of the game is balance. The portfolios that are recommended in this chapter contain between four and six different asset categories, which is sufficient to achieve a reasonable level of diversification without becoming unwieldy. The investment organizations included in your retirement plan may recommend more elaborate portfolios. Of course, there is certainly no harm in adding categories, but the objective here is to provide you with a strong foundation.

What are the six asset types that were evaluated by our optimization program? Each portfolio contains three types of stocks: large capitalization, small capitalization, and foreign stocks. As was discussed in Chapter 4, a blend of these three categories offers a higher return and less risk than plain vanilla U.S. stocks. More conservative investors may find it surprising that small capitalization and foreign stocks would be included in their portfolios, since they are considered risky. Don't forget, "risky" investments reduce the volatility of a portfolio if they have a low correlation with more traditional investments. Second, a bond fund has been included, which should serve as the debt component for investors who can tolerate a moderate level of volatility. Finally, stable value and money market funds were added for those nearing retirement—or for anyone else who cannot tolerate much volatility. These six categories were chosen due to their availability in most defined contribution plans and because various combinations of them should meet the needs of most investors. Later, you will receive some guidance for incorporating any other options that may be offered by your plan.

Risk and Return Forecasts

Since the computer will be searching for the best combination of risk and return, it is highly dependent on the quality of the forecasts for each category. In fact, optimization programs are very precise, which means that small differences in assumptions can meaningfully change the recommended portfolios. Of course, it is impossible to forecast risk and return with 100% accuracy, which could lead one to ask whether all of this technology is of any value. Keep in mind that any investment decision is based on forecasts of risk and return, whether you consciously make them or not. Therefore, why not explicitly make forecasts and use the best technology available to translate them into a sound portfolio structure?

Moreover, while we can't predict future returns with certainty, several factors should allow us to be in the ballpark. First, we have volumes of historical data on investment returns, and it is reasonable to begin with the assumption that the future will be similar to the past. Second, risk and return are determined by powerful economic forces that ensure that markets return to normal when they temporarily get out of whack. Finally, forecasting actual returns is less important than predicting the pattern of returns. For example, forecasting that stocks will outperform bonds is more important than predicting the exact results.

Table 4.2 (page 67) listed return assumptions ranging from 5% for money market funds to 12% for small capitalization and foreign stocks. In most cases, these forecasts are very similar to historical returns. However, the forecasts of returns on money market and bond funds exceed historical levels, although they are consistent with more recent experience. During most of this century, money market and bond investors demanded a return of 1% to 2% above the current level of inflation to compensate them for the risk that inflation could rise in the future. Having been burned by high inflation during the 1970s, bond investors now demand a spread of 2% to 4%. This accounts for the projected return on bonds of 7%, which compares with the long-run historical figure of 5.7%.

While someone could easily argue with one or more of these assumptions, most will find them both reasonable and internally consistent. Your retirement fund vendor will use its own assumptions to determine recommended portfolios, but the differences are likely to be relatively small.

Constraints

In theory, you should never place any constraints on the optimizer because the recommended portfolios could be inferior to other alternatives. But, as a practical matter, there is no value in devising a portfolio that most people find uncomfortable. Suppose the computer told you to invest your money as follows: 75% small capitalization stocks, 25% non–U.S. bonds. Would you actually invest in that portfolio? Probably not!

For this reason, most people place constraints on optimizers to ensure that the recommended portfolios are both familiar and comfortable. Typically, they place limitations on the allocation to less familiar options such as small capitalization and foreign stocks, and they require that the majority of the portfolio be committed to more traditional categories such as U.S. stocks, bonds, and money market funds. While constraints of this sort have been employed here, you will find that weightings have been allowed in small capitalization and foreign stocks to exceed the levels that are recommended by some market experts.

RECOMMENDED PORTFOLIOS

The four portfolios depicted in Table 6.1 (page 114) were developed using the optimization process that has been described. As discussed, the computer was restrained to generate recommendations that most people would find reasonably comfortable, and the suggested weightings were rounded to 5% intervals because a more precise structure would be unworkable for modest investors. Most people are understandably nervous about blindly following the advice of a computer model.

The four portfolios in Table 6.1 were developed by applying personal experience and judgment to the output of the optimization program. While each of these asset mixes contains a different blend of risk and return, you should understand that they are all "middle-of-the-road" portfolios. In other words, one could easily develop other alternatives at either end of the risk spectrum, but they would meet the needs of very few individuals.

Table 6.1

RECOMMENDED ASSET MIXES

% OF RETIREMENT PLAN

HIGHER RISK ⟵――――――⟶ LOWER RISK

CATEGORY	PORTFOLIO ONE	PORTFOLIO TWO	PORTFOLIO THREE	PORTFOLIO FOUR
Large Capitalization U.S. Stocks	30%	20%	20%	15%
Small Capitalization U.S. Stocks	30%	25%	20%	10%
Foreign Stocks	25%	20%	15%	10%
Bonds	15%	35%	35%	50%
Stable Value Funds	0%	0%	10%	10%
Money Market Funds	0%	0%	0%	5%
	100%	100%	100%	100%

Let's focus on the key elements of these structures. Portfolio One, which is the highest-risk alternative, has a total commitment to stocks of 85%. Equity exposure then decreases in stages from 65% in Portfolio Two to 35% in

Portfolio Four. Similarly, the allocations to small capitalization and foreign stocks are quite large in Portfolio One and gradually diminish in the remaining mixes. Not surprisingly, the two lower-risk portfolios have significant weightings in bonds, and Portfolio Four has a material commitment to stable value and money market funds.

If you are new to the investment world, you probably do not have any frame of reference to judge whether these portfolios are sensible. Each year, a consulting firm called Greenwich Associates surveys the 1,500 largest retirement, foundation, and endowment funds in the United States, which are managed by America's most experienced investment professionals. At the end of 1995, the average fund in this universe was structured as follows:

Table 6.2

STRUCTURE OF 1,500 LARGEST TAX-EXEMPT FUNDS

CATEGORY	% OF PORTFOLIO
U.S. Stocks	49.5%
Foreign Stocks	8.7%
Bonds	31.2%
Stable Value Funds	3.9%
Money Market Funds	3.5%
Other	3.2%
	100%

The average institutional fund is most comparable to recommended Portfolio Three, which is one of the moderate-risk alternatives. As you will note, total exposure to stocks is between 55% and 60% in both cases. Since the Greenwich Associates breakdown does not include a small capitalization category, the 49.5% weighting in U.S. stocks should be compared to the sum of the large and small capitalization stock categories in Portfolio Three, which is 40%. This points to the primary difference between the two portfolios: Portfolio Three provides less exposure to U.S. stocks and a 15% weighting in foreign stocks, as compared to 8.7% for the average fund. Actually, the larger and more sophisticated funds in the Greenwich Associates universe typically have a weighting of 15% to 20% in foreign stocks. Therefore, Portfolio Three is consistent with the largest institutional portfolios in the United States and is more diversified than many smaller funds. Portfolios One, Two, and Four are also similar to asset mixes with greater or lesser risk than are suggested by others.

WHICH PORTFOLIO IS RIGHT FOR YOU?

Chapter 5 discussed the four stages in the financial life cycle and suggested that a different level of risk was appropriate for each stage. Specifically, younger investors generally begin with more aggressive portfolios and then gradually decrease risk over the course of their lives. Consistent with this concept, here are some recommendations:

Table 6.3
RECOMMENDED PORTFOLIOS

STAGE	PORTFOLIO
Stage 1—Household Formation	One
Stage 2—Early Accumulation	Two
Stage 3—Maximum Accumulation	Three
Stage 4—Retirement	Four

Of course, these recommendations are designed for the average investor. Some individuals will not be able to tolerate the risk in even the most conservative alternative. At the other extreme, a few people will choose to maintain Portfolio One throughout their entire life. That is what makes retirement planning so interesting!

Recommended Portfolios

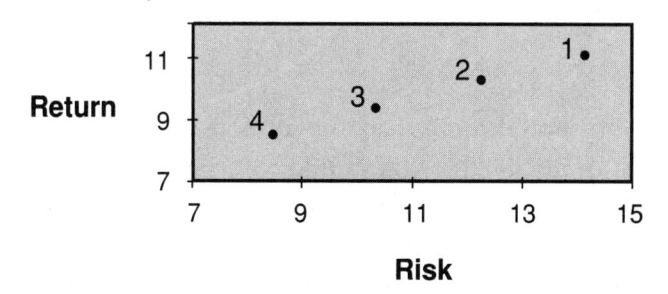

Chart 6.2

While you may be willing to accept these recommendations at face value, you probably are interested in some information on the risk and return that comes with each portfolio. Chart 6.2 provides a visual display of the risk/return tradeoff.

Now, let's focus on the actual projections of risk and return. You should recall that one of the important criteria for selecting a portfolio for your retirement plan is that it generates a return that will accomplish your objectives. Stated another way, you want to minimize the risk of coming up short. The long-term projected returns on each portfolio are as follows:

Table 6.4
PROJECTED ANNUAL RETURNS

Portfolio One	10.8%
Portfolio Two	10.0%
Portfolio Three	9.3%
Portfolio Four	8.3%

First, you should recall that the tables used to calculate the amount of money that you should contribute to your retirement plan assumed an average return of about 8%. Since all four of these portfolios should deliver that target, you might be tempted to select one of the lower-risk alternatives. However, you should note that Portfolios Three and Four do not provide a large margin for error. Another reason for considering one of the riskier alternatives is that a 1% or 2% increase in return will enhance your standard of living during retirement by 20% to 50%. Clearly, all four portfolios provide an expected return that is superior to lower-risk alternatives such as bond, stable value, and money market funds. What about risk?

Table 6.5
MEASURES OF RISK

	PORTFOLIO			
	ONE	TWO	THREE	FOUR
Probability of Loss in 1 Year	23%	21%	19%	17%
Probability of Loss>10%(1 Year)	7%	4%	3%	1%
Probability of Loss over 5 Years	5%	3%	3%	2%
Worst Year in 100	-20%	-16%	-14%	-11%

The historical data included in Chapter 5 indicated that bonds and stocks suffer losses between 25% and 30% of the time. Because of their diversification, the four recommended portfolios should decline in value less frequently and the size of those declines is likely to be more modest. As you will note, even the most aggressive portfolio should suffer a loss greater than 10% in only seven out of one hundred years. Similarly, all four portfolios offer a very small probability of a negative return over a five-year period. Finally, the worst-case loss of 20% on the most aggressive portfolio is less than half of the 44% loss that was actually experienced by stocks in 1931. Needless to say, a 20% loss is painful, but it should occur in only one of every one hundred years. Perhaps you will be lucky enough to avoid that year in your investing lifetime. While all four portfolios entail more volatility than money market or stable value funds, this volatility is both manageable and justified by the extra return.

After you've digested all of this data, you will have to decide which of these alternatives is right for you. The trade-offs should be very clear. Portfolio One provides a large return advantage, but it is subject to losses over short periods of time. In contrast, Portfolio Four is relatively immune to major losses, but its modest projected return will make it more difficult to achieve your retirement objectives. If the portfolio recommended for your stage in life seems too risky, simply move one notch down the risk scale. However, don't lose sight of the fact that all four of these alternatives represent diversified portfolios that entail a moderate level of risk.

WHERE DOES COMPANY STOCK FIT IN?

Earlier, it was noted that allocating a portion of your retirement fund to your company's own stock is risky, because both your current income and retirement security are then dependent on the fortunes of the company. But, assuming that you choose to invest in company stock, where does it fit in?

One approach is to allocate it to the appropriate category within the recommended portfolio. In other words, you incorporate the company stock into your asset allocation. Suppose you select Portfolio One, which calls for a 30% weighting in large capitalization stocks. Further, assume that you invest 10% of your fund in company stock, which also has a large capitalization. In this case, your allocation to large capitalization stocks would consist of a 10% weighting in company stock and a 20% commitment to a large capitalization stock mutual fund. If your company has a market capitalization of $5 billion or less, then it would be incorporated into the small capitalization stock allocation.

The other approach is to ignore the dollars that you commit to company stock for the purposes of asset allocation. In this case, the company stock is viewed as a separate investment and the rest of the portfolio is structured as if it did not exist. Once again, suppose you designate 10% of your fund for company stock. You would then allocate the remaining 90% of your dollars according to the percentages shown in Table 6.1 (page 114). Table 6.6, below, compares the two alternatives:

Table 6.6
COMPANY STOCK

CATEGORY	ALTERNATIVE ONE	ALTERNATIVE TWO
Company Stock	10%	10%
Large Capitalization Stocks	20%	27%
Small Capitalization Stocks	30%	27%
Foreign Stocks	25%	22.5%
Bonds	15%	13.5%
Total	100%	100%

As you will note, the differences in weightings are fairly modest, and the returns are likely to be fairly similar. Therefore, you should choose the approach that is easier for you to understand and implement.

HOW DO YOU DEAL WITH OTHER ASSET TYPES?

It is entirely possible that your plan offers investment categories other than the six that are included in the four recommended portfolios. How do you adjust the recommended weightings to accommodate them?

The best solution is to run an optimization program with the broader list of asset types. Your mutual fund vendor undoubtedly has a variety of recommended portfolios including both simple and complex structures, and their suggestions are likely to be consistent with those in this chapter. As was mentioned earlier, some vendors are willing to work with you to customize a portfolio to meet your needs. If these resources are not available, then you can use good old common sense to adjust the recommendations in this book.

For example, suppose you are generally comfortable with Portfolio Two but decide to allocate 5% of your plan to a non–U.S. bond fund. Since this category was not included in our lineup, where does it fit? Portfolio Two called for a 35% allocation to bonds, which suggests that you simply invest 30% in the domestic bond fund to complement the 5% that was allocated to the foreign fund. Therefore, the overall portfolio structure is unchanged; it simply enjoys more diversification than the basic asset mix detailed in Table 6.1. Suppose you want to invest 10% of your money in a very focused stock portfolio, such as a Technology Sector Fund. In this case, the 10% allocation would be funded by reducing your 25% weighting in small capitalization stock funds to 15%.

It is also possible that your plan does not contain all of the basic investment categories that were included in Table

6.1 (page 114). Once again, you deal with this problem by using common sense to adjust the recommendations. For example, assuming that your plan does not have a small capitalization stock fund, you would reallocate those funds to another domestic stock fund in order to maintain the overall stock/bond mix.

Asset allocation is not an exact science. The recommended asset mixes in this chapter are meant to serve as a guide, not as the final word. You should feel free to adjust them to meet your personal interests and preferences.

GETTING FROM HERE TO THERE

At this point, you have decided how much risk you want to take and have selected the asset allocation that seems best suited to meet your needs. The odds are pretty good that your current portfolio is very different from the recommended asset allocation that you selected. How do you get from here to there?

A cardinal rule of finance is that you should avoid making sudden changes in your investments. A better alternative is to gradually move from your current position to the recommended weightings. For example, you might shift in twelve monthly increments, four quarterly installments, or any other similar scheme.

What is wrong with acting quickly? Assume that all of your assets are currently invested in a stable value fund and that you accept the recommendation to move into a diversified portfolio with exposure to stocks of 65%. Now, suppose that the stock market declines 10% right after you move 65% of your hard-earned dollars into stock mutual funds.

(Remember Murphy's Law, which says that anything that can go wrong will go wrong!) The odds are that you move back to the stable value fund and swear off stocks forever. This is exactly the kind of emotional decision that an organized approach to investing is designed to avoid. In contrast, a gradual transition will average the highs and lows, which will give you added confidence in your investment program.

LIFESTYLE FUNDS

If constructing your own portfolio seems like a lot of work, you may want to consider **lifestyle mutual funds**, which are now offered by many of the major fund sponsors. A lifestyle or life cycle fund is a balanced portfolio that invests in a number of different asset classes, with an asset mix that is targeted to people in a specific age group and a specific stage in life. For example, an aggressive lifestyle fund would be heavily oriented toward stocks in order to meet the needs of younger investors.

Typically, a fund sponsor offers three or four lifestyle funds to meet the needs of investors of all ages. Lifestyle funds represent one-stop shopping, because an individual simply purchases one fund, which is held until the next stage in the life cycle. At that point, he switches to the next fund, which has a more conservative asset mix.

The great advantage of lifestyle funds is simplicity. However, there are several drawbacks. First, you lose control of your asset mix and are forced to accept the risk level dictated by the fund. Second, you are forced to accept the portfolio managers that the organization assigns to each of the asset classes held in the lifestyle fund. In other words, you lose the ability to mix and match funds.

ALLOCATING YOUR CONTRIBUTIONS

While selecting an asset mix is the most important decision that you will make, you have two other jobs that need to be completed in order to fully implement your investment program. First, you must select insurance products or mutual funds in each asset category from the menu offered by your retirement plan. Chapter 7 covers the initial selection of funds, as well as the ongoing evaluation of the performance of the funds that you hold. Your other responsibility is to allocate your contributions in a way that ensures that your retirement plan remains on track.

The actual asset allocation of your retirement plan will drift away from the targets over time, because the investment categories held in your portfolio will generate different rates of return. As an example, consider a simple portfolio that is initially divided equally between stocks and bonds. During the year, stocks earn a return of 20% while bonds earn 10%. At year end, stocks will represent 52% of the portfolio and bonds 48%. You might reasonably view this difference as insignificant. But if this trend continues unchecked for ten years, stocks will constitute more than 70% of the portfolio. Clearly, a portfolio with equity exposure of 70% has very different risk characteristics from one with an equal balance between stocks and bonds. Assuming that you chose the fifty-fifty mix carefully, 70% exposure should be unacceptable.

In order to counteract this tendency to drift, most investors periodically rebalance their portfolio. Rebalancing is simply the act of returning the weights to the initial targets. In the above example, the investor would transfer 2% of his portfolio from stocks to bonds, which would bring the weightings back to the original levels.

Since you are making regular contributions to your retirement fund, you can rebalance without having to sell any of your investments. In other words, you can direct your contributions among the various components in order to restore the proper balance. Assume, for example, that you began the year 1995 with $20,000 invested according to Portfolio Two. Based on the actual returns for the year, the beginning and ending values would appear as follows:

Table 6.7

	Beginning 1995 $	%	Return	Ending 1995 $	%
Large Capitalization Stocks	4,000	20	37.4%	5,496	21.2
Small Capitalization Stocks	5,000	25	34.5	6,725	26.0
Foreign Stocks	4,000	20	11.2	4,448	17.2
Bonds	7,000	35	31.7	9,219	35.6
Total	$20,000	100%		$25,888	100%

First, you should note that this was a banner year in that the portfolio increased in value from $20,000 to $25,888, or 29.4%. However, the actual weightings in several categories now differ modestly from the target, and the allocation to foreign securities is 2.8% shy of the objective. We will also assume that you intend to contribute $3,000 to the portfolio. In order to rebalance, the contribution should be allocated as follows:

Table 6.8

	ACTUAL BALANCE	%	$	TARGET CONTRIBUTION
Large Capitalization Stocks	$5,496	20	$5,778	$282
Small Capitalization Stocks	6,725	25	7,222	497
Foreign Stocks	4,448	20	5,778	1,330
Bonds	9,219	35	10,110	891
Total	$25,888	100	$28,888*	$3,000

*Ending value plus $3,000 contribution

Almost one-half of the contribution is allocated to the foreign stock category in order to bring it back into line. This demonstrates a subtle but important feature of rebalancing, which is that it allocates funds to investments that have performed poorly. In this case, foreign stocks returned just over 11% during the year, as compared to more than 30% for the other categories. Because rebalancing represents a disciplined means of "buying low and selling high," it may increase the return on your portfolio in addition to keeping the weightings near the target.

This example is actually somewhat unrealistic, because it assumes that you make your entire annual contribution at one time. In fact, most people contribute to their retirement fund through a monthly payroll reduction. How does this affect the rebalancing process? If your actual portfolio weightings are in line with the targets, the allocation of your contribution among each category should be the same as the target weighting. For example, 20% of your monthly contribution would be directed to large capitalization stocks assuming that you are using Portfolio Two, which calls for a 20% weighting in that category.

A reasonable approach to rebalancing is to value your retirement fund about twice a year and to compare the actual weightings with the targets. The categories that are particularly underweighted then receive more than their fair share of the contributions for the next six months. In the above example, foreign stocks would normally receive 20% of the contributions. Because the actual weighting in this category is below the target, you could allocate 25% of contributions to it for the next six months, which means that each of the other asset types would receive a reduced share. At the next review date, you would analyze the portfolio again and adjust the contributions as required.

If this approach seems like too much work, another method is to consistently allocate your contributions according to the target weightings. In other words, the allocation of your contributions never changes. Instead, once or twice a year, you compare the actual weightings to the targets and then buy and sell within each category as required. While this method is fairly straightforward, you should recall that mutual fund sponsors and insurance companies often levy exit charges, which could render it impractical.

Rebalancing is an imperfect art, because the portfolio is a moving target. Therefore, regardless of the rebalancing scheme that you employ, you will never exactly achieve the target weightings. The objective is to stay close enough to the targets so that the portfolio delivers the risk/return characteristics you desire.

MOVING FROM ONE STAGE TO THE NEXT

According to the life cycle approach to asset allocation, you should require only about four portfolio structures over the course of your investing life. Once you have created the right portfolio for your current stage, a little bit of annual maintenance is required to keep things on track. Otherwise, you simply stick with the program for the next ten to twenty years, which is the length of each stage. But what happens as you approach the next stage in life? In other words, how do you transition from one portfolio to the next?

One answer is to simply wait until the end of the stage and then adjust the portfolio in one fell swoop. Since each successive portfolio has less exposure to stocks, you simply make a one-time reduction in your equity exposure and transfer the proceeds to bond, stable value, and money market funds as required. Other than periodic rebalancing, you could then focus on golf for the next ten to twenty years.

While this is certainly the easiest approach, it is fraught with peril. Suppose that you decide to make this transition following a downdraft in the market. Most of us become more cautious with age, so it would be very easy to decide that stocks are no longer appropriate for you following some market turmoil. This situation is a textbook example of a permanent loss, because the decrease in equity exposure makes it very difficult to recoup the temporary decline in stock prices.

A better way to transition from one stage to the next is to accomplish the shift over a period of years. For example, suppose your retirement fund has a 65% allocation to stocks and the recommended portfolio for the next stage calls for a 50% weighting. A sensible approach is to reduce your equity exposure by 3% per year during each of the last five years of your current stage in the life cycle. This transition can be accomplished by actually selling stocks or by allocating new contributions toward bonds and stable value funds.

THE PERILS OF MARKET TIMING

The basic thrust of this chapter is that an individual should carefully create a diversified portfolio that remains relatively unchanged until the next stage in life. Even then, the shifts in asset allocation are both modest and gradual. This "hands-off" approach to investing conflicts with the "wheel-and-deal" mentality that is so common on Wall Street. As you know, market newsletters and the financial press are filled with recommendations as to the best place to invest your money today, and these recommendations tend to change frequently. An active strategy of moving money between stocks, bonds, and other securities is called **market timing**.

The basic premise of market timing is that each type of investment experiences periods of high and low returns. For example, stocks outperform bonds in most periods, but there are certainly times when bonds provide the better return. The objective of market timing is to concentrate your money in the category that is on the verge of experiencing the positive leg of the cycle. Once that leg in the cycle runs its course, you rotate to the next category.

Market timing actually offers huge potential to build wealth. An individual who invested $100 in the Standard and Poors 500 at the beginning of 1901 would have been worth $733,383 at the end of 1995. This ignores the effect of taxes and assumes that all dividends were reinvested. However, had he been out of the market during the three worst years, the $100 would have grown to $2,830,704. Wow! Just a couple of good market calls would have allowed him to increase his wealth by a factor of four.

Before you embark on a career in market timing, though, be forewarned: a recent study found that you would have earned a return of zero had you missed the best 55 of the 780 months between 1926 and 1990. Despite being invested in stocks 93% of the time, you missed all of the rise in stock prices by making a small number of poor timing decisions.

The moral of the story is clear. If you are going to attempt to time the markets, either you or your advisers had better be right. Of course, no one is right or wrong all of the time, so the question is whether someone can achieve a good enough batting average to make market timing worthwhile. You won't be surprised to learn that people who are in the market timing business claim they are successful, and there are a number of instances in which market gurus have made good calls. But no one has been able to produce a carefully documented study that demonstrates successful market timing over a long period of time.

Not only is market timing of questionable value, it can also be very risky. Because the return on stocks comes in spurts, being in or out of the market at the wrong time can be quite painful. Another consideration is that market timing can be expensive. As will be discussed in the next chapter, some mutual funds and insurance products levy sales or surrender charges, which could easily eliminate any advantage gained from a successful market judgment. The bottom line is simple. Set up your portfolio carefully. Rebalance it periodically. Otherwise, leave it alone!

Suppose you choose to ignore this advice because of the huge returns that market timing can theoretically generate. What is the best way to inject a little bit of timing into your fund?

Market timers are often unsuccessful because their emotions tend to cloud their judgment. In order to deal with this problem, many investment firms have developed computerized approaches to market timing that are offered through asset allocation mutual funds. These funds rely on sophisticated valuation models that process objective data while keeping human judgment to a minimum. While the track records of these funds are mixed, they are superior to the "seat-of-the-pants" alternative. If you must time the markets, a reasonable approach is to allocate a portion of your retirement plan (say, 20%) to one of these funds. If the fund does achieve good results, it will enhance the return on your overall plan. On the other hand, a modest weighting will ensure that you do not get clobbered because your market timer zigged when it should have zagged.

ALCHEMY

Because asset allocation is so important, this chapter covered a lot of material and necessitated the use of a large number of charts and tables. But the extra effort that you devote to understanding this concept will pay off, because asset allocation will make or break your retirement program.

Asset allocation is not an exact science, and reasonable people disagree on the details of creating and maintaining portfolios. However, most informed observers of the investment world *do* agree on a few principles that are both basic and powerful. First, diversified portfolios offer a "free lunch" because they significantly reduce risk without sacrificing much return. Second, "all-or-nothing" investment decisions are dangerous, which suggests that any changes in strategy should be implemented in stages. Third, market timing is likely to be nonproductive and is potentially dangerous. Most people are better served by maintaining their asset mix through thick and thin. Finally, nothing in this chapter is carved in stone. The portfolio weightings and rebalancing schemes that were recommended should serve as guidelines that you should feel free to adapt to your own circumstances.

You have now completed most of the steps in an organized investment program. At this point, you have identified your retirement objective and have calculated the amount that you must save to reach that goal. After a bit of soul searching, you came to grips with investment risk and selected an asset allocation that seems likely to deliver the right balance between risk and return. Finally, you know how to adjust your portfolio over the course of your life as your needs change. All that remains is to select individual mutual funds or insurance products and to monitor them over time to ensure that they are performing as expected.

Key Points to Remember

- Optimal portfolios deliver the highest rate of return for the risk involved.
- Rational investors always choose optimal portfolios because others are inferior.
- Once you identify your optimal portfolio, avoid the temptation to tinker with it.

CHAPTER 7

Selecting Mutual Funds and Insurance Products

> *The investor who wants to make an intelligent commitment in mutual fund shares has thus a large and somewhat bewildering variety of choices before him.*
>
> —BENJAMIN GRAHAM
> THE INTELLIGENT INVESTOR, 1973

Benjamin Graham was a famous investor and the author of several of the most enduring books in the field, including *The Intelligent Investor*. Given that more than 6,000 mutual funds are now available, it is very humorous that his statement regarding the "large and somewhat bewildering variety" of mutual funds was made at a time when only 356 were in existence. If Ben Graham was bewildered, then we must be totally lost!

How in the world does anyone select a small number of funds from among this incredible number of options? In addition to the sheer number of funds, investors are subjected to a tremendous amount of hype and self-promotion by mutual fund vendors. The financial press is filled with ads for mutual funds that claim to have the best performance in their category, and a variety of publications rank mutual funds, often with different results. Finally, mutual fund managers turn over rapidly, and funds often modify their investment strategy in response to a period of below-par performance. Therefore, selecting a good fund is just the first step in a process that involves ongoing monitoring and review.

The only way to overcome all of these hurdles is to go about the process of selecting a fund in an organized manner. This chapter discusses the factors that you should consider when evaluating funds and proposes a step-by-step process to actually make your selections.

MATCHING FUNDS AND ASSET CLASSES

The portfolios that were recommended in Chapter 6 contained between four and six different asset classes. Since balanced funds generally invest in three or four of these classes, you may be able to get away with selecting only one or two additional funds if you include a balanced fund in your lineup. However, if you follow the advice to avoid balanced funds due to the loss of control, then you will have to select between four and six funds for your retirement portfolio.

The first problem that you face is matching the funds that are available through your plan to the asset classes that are included in the recommended portfolios. For example, how do you know which of the funds available through your plan invests in small capitalization stocks?

Unfortunately, categorizing mutual funds is not quite as easy as you might think. First, the guidelines that govern the management of any given fund can be quite broad, which means that the portfolio manager is allowed to invest in a wide array of securities. A classic example of this problem occurred in 1996 when the most famous U.S. stock fund, the Magellan Fund, invested almost 20% of its assets in long-term Treasury bonds.

Where does such a fund fit in the recommended asset mix? Is it a large capitalization stock fund, a bond fund, or what? Beyond this confusion, the real difficulty in categorizing funds arises from the fact that the mutual fund industry has not adopted uniform labels to describe funds. For example, a fund investing in small capitalization stocks could be labeled "growth," "aggressive growth," or "small company," depending upon the source of information. Additionally, many funds have names such as Magellan, Windsor, or New Horizons that don't tell you anything about the fund's investment strategy.

There are two solutions to the classification problem. First, you can do some homework on each of the funds available through your retirement plan in order to gain a basic understanding of the investment approach that is employed. The majority of this chapter is devoted to understanding a fund's investment philosophy and the results that it has achieved. Second, you can select an index fund, which will make the job very easy.

INDEX FUNDS

An index fund is a mutual fund that takes a completely passive approach to investing in securities, since it attempts to simply match the return on a market index. For example, a Standard and Poors 500 Index fund purchases and holds all 500 stocks that make up the index, and it delivers a return equal to the index return less the cost of managing the fund. (The cost is very low, because running an index fund is a mechanical process.) In contrast, actively managed stock and bond funds attempt to outperform the market and the competition through good security selection, market timing, or trading skill. During a given year, stock mutual funds buy and sell as much as 75% of the value of the fund, while bond funds turn over the entire fund as often as twice. All of this trading activity is designed to gain a leg up on the competition.

A debate has been raging for more than twenty-five years as to the merits of active versus passive management. In one corner are mutual fund managers, fund evaluation services, and most fund participants, who believe that an intelligent, resourceful portfolio manager should be able to outperform his peers. This group favors active management and is willing to pay relatively high fees in an attempt to outperform the market. At the other extreme are those who argue that it is difficult, if not impossible, to consistently beat the competition, so a better solution is to simply join them by investing in the entire market. The following should shed a little light on this contentious issue.

Large institutional investors such as mutual funds now own more than 50% of all stocks and bonds, and they account for 70% to 80% of trading activity. In other words, they *are* the market. Since mutual funds are the market, it stands to reason that the average fund should earn the market return before taking into account the costs of managing the fund. Therefore, the average fund should deliver a net return equal to the market return less expenses. For example, the typical large capitalization stock fund should underperform the S&P 500 by about 1.4% per year, since that is the annual cost of operating the average fund. In fact, study after study of mutual fund performance has confirmed this result. Just to mention one, the mutual fund evaluation service Morningstar, Inc., found that only 14% of diversified equity mutual funds beat the S&P 500 during the ten years from 1986 through 1995. While all of this may seem academic, the implications are very important. The average retirement plan participant who invests in the average fund is wasting money, because he could achieve better results by choosing an index fund.

Most experts acknowledge that the average fund will underperform an index fund over time, but they argue that a small number of funds will be able to consistently beat the market. Do some funds consistently beat the competition? In fact, a small number of funds have been able to consistently outperform the averages but that number will always remain small due to the effects of competition. Capital markets in the United States and other industrialized countries are highly competitive, with a large number of well-informed participants. In this environment, it is very difficult for any single investor to maintain an edge over the competition for long, because others will imitate his strategy, which will destroy its effectiveness. While a few funds can be expected to rise above the crowd, it is exceedingly difficult to identify them in advance. Luck is a very important contributor to fund returns over the short term, which means that a good track record over the past few years is not an indicator that a fund is among the chosen few.

The bottom line is that very few funds outperform the market over time, and it is quite difficult to identify them in advance. Besides, everyone else is trying to find them as well. Moreover, a fund managed by a portfolio manager with the "Midas touch" is likely to experience huge cash inflows, which may force a change in investment strategy. Finally, successful portfolio managers get very rich and are subject to burnout at an early age. So, even if you find a great fund, the odds are not very good that the performance will last.

Pros and Cons of Index Funds

It is hoped that this discussion has convinced you that index funds are worthy of your consideration, because they are likely to outperform the other investment options available to you. There are two other advantages to index funds that you also should understand. First, index funds are very diversified, because they hold most if not all of the securities in the index. This diversification ensures that the return on the fund will be very similar to that of the index. In contrast, actively managed funds can dramatically underperform the market if the portfolio manager makes a large bet that proves incorrect.

Why is it important that your returns track the index? The risk and return data on each of the four recommended asset mixes in Chapter 6 assumed that you earned the market return in each asset class. If you dramatically underperform in any given category, the actual risk on the portfolio may be greater than was indicated. Second, index funds are pure investments in that the fund does not stray into other types of securities. For example, a small capitalization stock index fund holds only small capitalization stocks. This eliminates the classification problem that was discussed above.

The major drawback of an index fund is that it will never be the best-performing fund in a given category. In fact, in any given quarter or year, a number of actively managed funds will outperform the index, which may give you the feeling that you are being left behind. But the bets that allowed those funds to outperform are likely to prove wrong in subsequent periods, which means that the index fund will outperform all but a few funds over time. Once again, it is very difficult to identify these funds in advance, but many people want to try.

Setting Up an Indexed Retirement Portfolio

Depending upon the vendor, your retirement plan may or may not offer index funds. Further, mutual fund sponsors do not always offer index funds in every category. However, if index funds are available, as many as four of the six asset classes in the recommended portfolios may be represented: large capitalization stocks, small capitalization stocks, foreign stocks, and bonds. Indexed stable value and money market funds do not exist.

How do you know an index fund when you see it? Each index fund will be described by the market index that is used as the benchmark. For example, large capitalization stock index funds are generally designed to match the S&P

500. The corresponding market index for each category is as follows:

CATEGORY	MARKET INDEX
Large Capitalization Stocks	S&P 500
Small Capitalization Stocks	Russell 2000 Index
Foreign Stocks	Europe, Australia, Far East Index (EAFE)
Bonds	Lehman Government/Corporate Index

The description of the fund in its marketing literature will include clear language indicating that the fund is designed to match the specified market index. For example, a small capitalization stock index fund might be called a Russell 2000 Fund. Index funds exist in a number of other categories, but focusing on the primary asset classes keeps the issue simple.

Suppose your plan offers index funds from several different vendors. How do you choose among them? The only factor that you need to consider is cost. Since the return on an index fund is equal to the index return less expenses, the fund with the lowest cost will win. The annual cost of operating a fund is called the **expense ratio,** and it must be disclosed in the fund's prospectus. As a rule, larger index funds have lower expense ratios, because they are able to spread their costs over a larger base.

The simplest approach to structuring your retirement plan is to index all four categories. If you chose either Portfolio Three or Four, then you must also select stable value and money market funds. Most plans only offer one option in each of these categories, which makes the choice simple.

If you are not completely persuaded by the arguments in favor of index funds, does it make sense to index just one or two categories? The most competitive category of investment is arguably the market for large capitalization stocks in the United States, since they are carefully evaluated by hundreds of research analysts. Therefore it is particularly difficult for any single investor to gain an edge over the competition in this category, which suggests that an index fund represents a very attractive alternative. A reasonable strategy for those who want to attempt to beat the market is to index the large capitalization category and to invest the remainder of the portfolio in actively managed funds that seek to outperform less developed markets.

While the arguments in favor of indexing are pretty powerful, only about 20% of investment dollars are allocated to index funds. Clearly, most people want to try to beat the market even though they know that the odds are against them. While there is no guarantee that you will be successful, the remainder of this chapter is devoted to the factors that you should consider when selecting actively managed funds.

AN OVERVIEW OF MUTUAL FUND SELECTION

Mutual fund evaluation is a blend of art and science that involves both quantitative and qualitative factors. While many criteria should be considered, they can easily be summarized by five words that begin with the letter P: People, Philosophy, Process, Price, and Performance. You might initially respond that it is impossible for the average person to evaluate the "Five P's" for a given mutual fund, much less to compare funds according to these criteria. In fact, many excellent mutual fund evaluation services are now available, making the job much more manageable. Let's consider each of the P's in some detail.

People/Organization

While financial technology has advanced considerably in recent years, investment management remains an art form, which means that people are very important. In fact, the quality of an investment organization and the quality of its employees are almost one and the same. Of course, you can't personally get to know the investment professionals who are managing a fund, but it is possible to make some judgments about the quality of an organization and its employees. Why don't we consider organizational issues first.

The level of resources that an organization commands is very important, and a large mutual fund sponsor that offers a variety of funds is likely to be better positioned than a smaller organization. For example, a larger fund group can afford economists, research analysts, computer databases, and other tools that make portfolio managers more effective. Similarly, a variety of mutual fund offerings requires a larger group of portfolio managers who can share ideas, which may enhance the performance of any given fund. For example, the manager of an international stock fund may be able to provide unique insights into the competitive position of U.S. companies, which could give the domestic stock fund manager an edge over the competition.

Second, large or prestigious funds get special attention from both corporate management and Wall Street. Senior executives of companies make special trips to important fund managers to discuss corporate strategy and the outlook for the company. Of course, management is not allowed to divulge inside information, but these meetings provide the opportunity for in-depth discussion and analysis. Portfolio managers of "lesser" funds are also able to gain access to corporate management, but these contacts occur in large group meetings. Brokerage firms also give preference to their most important institutional customers in the form of access to their research departments and trading desks.

The fact that a mutual fund sponsor is included in your retirement plan generally means that your employer has done a careful review of the quality of the organization and its reputation. As an additional check, you might review one of the many services and publications that evaluate mutual funds. Several of these rate the overall quality of a mutual fund sponsor in addition to the individual funds that it offers. While a good rating certainly does not guarantee good results, it *does* suggest that a fund group is highly regarded.

While the size and clout of an organization can be important, this discussion was not intended to be a commercial for the large mutual fund groups. Many of the best-performing funds are offered by smaller sponsors; in fact, the relative performance of stock funds often decreases with size. This occurs for two reasons. First, larger funds tend to buy larger stocks, which penalizes returns since smaller stocks tend to outperform over time. Second, a large fund often moves the price of a stock whenever it enters the market, which also acts as a drag. In the final analysis, the key factor that determines the success of a fund is the quality of the fund manager. People make the difference!

The first thing that you should find out about a fund is how long its manager has been at the helm. Luckily, this information is prominently displayed for each fund in services such as Morningstar and Value Line. Why is the manager's tenure so important? As previously mentioned, managing money is an art, which means that each investment manager develops his or her own style. Additionally, successful managers develop a certain chemistry with the organization's other portfolio managers and research analysts. For both of these reasons, a fund's track record is relevant only if the person responsible for that record continues to manage the fund. When a new manager assumes responsibility for a fund, there is no guarantee of success even if she had a good record at another organization. Therefore, you should have a strong bias toward funds in which the manager has been in place for a number of years. As a popular saying goes, what you see is what you get. How long a tenure is long enough? A bare minimum is a market cycle, which is generally three to five years, and a longer period is preferable.

Mutual fund managers have been successful using a variety of different investment approaches. However, all top managers have one thing in common: they develop a well-articulated investment philosophy that they stick with during good times and bad.

Investment Philosophy

A domestic equity fund manager has approximately 7,000 stocks to choose from, and bond investors also face a dizzying number of alternatives. How in the world does anyone select a manageable number of securities from this universe?

The answer is that each investor must develop selection criteria. In other words, she must have strong ideas about the factors that cause one type of security to outperform another, and she should purchase only securities that display those factors. These attributes form the core of an investment philosophy. Investment philosophies fall into and out of favor, which means that even the most skilled managers suffer periods of poor performance. However, the worst mistake of all is to attempt to flit from one strategy to the next. Investors who lack a well-defined approach are the proverbial generals fighting the last war and are doomed to failure. In order to equip you to evaluate potential funds, the next section will consider both stock and bond investment approaches.

Equity Investment Philosophies

Virtually all stock mutual fund managers use one or the other or a combination of two basic equity approaches. The **growth** philosophy is based on the belief that the stocks of companies that are growing very rapidly deliver higher returns to investors. Growth stock managers look for companies that are experiencing rapid growth in sales, earnings, and dividends. Typically, these companies are found in industries that are growing rapidly, such as technology, health care, and specialty retailing. Because of their growth, such companies are interesting to follow and exciting to own. Indeed, some of America's great fortunes were built by those who had the insight to buy and hold growth companies. However, growth stocks can be very volatile because they usually sell at relatively high prices. Investors are willing to pay a premium for rapid growth and financial strength. But these high valuations provide no room for error. When a growth company reports disappointing earnings or hints at a slowdown in growth, its stock often declines significantly. These stocks have been labeled "torpedo stocks," because they sink like a damaged ship in response to bad news.

The polar opposite of growth stock investing is the **value approach,** which is based on the belief that good returns result from buying stocks at bargain prices. Wall Street is characterized by fads in which some types of companies are in vogue while others are totally ignored. Value investors attempt to find good companies that are temporarily out of favor. By definition, value stocks are emotionally difficult to purchase because of their unpopularity. Value stocks generally have relatively little downside risk, because they have already been punished by the market. The primary drawback of value stocks is that they are often mature companies in unexciting industries. Moreover, value stocks sometimes remain cheap for a long period of time.

Should you pick a growth- or a value-oriented stock fund for your retirement portfolio? The answer is that it does not really matter, because both approaches have delivered similar returns over long periods of time. The key is to select a fund with a clear orientation that it has held over time. How do you know which funds fit this description? First, you can read the "Investment Objectives and Guidelines" section of the fund's prospectus. Unfortunately, these documents are pretty dry and are filled with confusing investment jargon. A much easier solution is to check one of the evaluation services, such as Morningstar, which are found in the business section of many public libraries. Each stock fund is categorized according to the following grid:

	Growth	Blend	Value
Large Cap			
Medium Cap			
Small Cap			

Chart 7.1

One of the six boxes will be highlighted to indicate the fund's approach to selecting stocks and the size of the companies that it purchases. In order to determine whether the fund has consistently followed this approach, this information is also presented for each of the past five to seven years.

BOND INVESTMENT

The risk and return on a bond fund is largely a function of two factors: the quality of the bonds held and their average maturity. As was discussed in Chapter 4, longer-term bonds are much more volatile than short-term securities and they usually deliver a higher return. Similarly, lower-quality issues are more volatile than blue chips, because they are subject to default. Not surprisingly, junk bonds deliver a higher return over time, but they are subject to poor short-term results. As was the case with stocks, Morningstar uses a grid to evaluate each bond fund:

	Short	Intermediate	Long
High Quality			
Medium Quality			
Low Quality			

Chart 7.2

Once again, one of the six boxes will be highlighted, providing you with a clear indication of the type of bonds that the fund buys.

FUND SIZE

Larger mutual funds generally have lower expense ratios, because they are able to spread their costs over a larger asset base. On the other hand, investment performance may be negatively impacted as a fund grows, since it becomes more difficult to manage. The optimal size of a mutual fund is related to the fund's investment philosophy and to the type of securities that it purchases. Because the bond markets are large and quite liquid, a large asset base is generally positive for a bond fund because of the cost advantage. Similarly, a fund that invests in large capitalization stocks has a large number of liquid securities from which to choose. However, small capitalization stock funds run into trouble as they grow because they can't invest very much money in any single small company, which makes it difficult to effectively deploy their assets. To deal with this problem, they are forced to invest in larger companies. Alternatively, they include more holdings in the portfolio, which usually means that they resort to a more superficial level of analysis of each company. Both of these factors can impact returns. How big is too big? In general, you should be wary of a small capitalization fund with more than $5 billion in assets—an optimum size is closer to $1 billion.

FUNKY SECURITIES

Since most people cannot bring themselves to actually read a mutual fund prospectus, they are unaware that many fund managers are given a great deal of latitude to invest the fund as they see fit. This flexibility creates two potential problems. First, the manager may invest in a variety of stocks and bonds, which makes it difficult to place the fund in the proper category in your portfolio structure. Second, many funds are allowed to invest in esoteric derivative securities. In 1994, several funds sustained significant losses when these securities plummeted in value due to rising interest rates. While derivatives have a place in some portfolios, one of the fundamental tenets of this book is that most investors should keep it simple, which means that complex securities are to be avoided. In response to this problem, a portion of the Morningstar report on each fund is devoted to its use of derivatives. Check this section to make sure that the fund is following a plain vanilla investment philosophy that makes minimal use of esoterica.

Currency

The final topic under the heading of investment philosophy applies only to international stock and bond funds. Specifically, what is the fund's philosophy with regard to hedging against currency fluctuations?

This is a complex subject on which both academics and practitioners disagree. When a U.S. investor purchases a foreign security, he must convert dollars into the currency of that country in order to consummate the trade. When the security is sold, he must then convert the proceeds back into dollars. Therefore, his return is dependent on both the return on that security and any change in the value of the currency versus the dollar. If the dollar falls versus other currencies, the return on his investment will be enhanced, and a rise in the dollar decreases return. An investor who wishes to avoid exposure to currency fluctuations can hedge his position in the foreign exchange market.

Should a fund hedge its currency exposure or not? Briefly, the evidence suggests that funds that do not hedge earn higher returns, although they are more volatile due to the currency fluctuations. Funds that fully hedge earn lower returns due to the cost of hedging, but they are much more stable. Which approach makes more sense? Probably a compromise that is practiced by many funds, in which the portfolio manager does not hedge unless he has a very strong view that a given currency is likely to fall significantly versus the dollar. This approach minimizes the cost of hedging while also keeping volatility within reasonable limits. Once again, Morningstar and other services discuss the currency policy of each international fund.

Process

A well-defined investment philosophy is of no value unless it is actually implemented in the portfolio, which means that the portfolio manager's judgments must be translated into purchases and sales that are executed on a timely basis. Simply stated, every investment manager must have a process.

As an outsider, you don't have an opportunity to examine the fund manager's modus operandi directly. Therefore, you are forced to rely on two indirect measures. First, you can have some confidence that the portfolio manager is well organized if the fund consistently falls in the same box on the investment philosophy grid discussed above. Another favorable indicator is a pattern of investment performance that is consistently in line with other funds following the same investment approach. Both of these indicate a finely honed investment strategy that is implemented on a disciplined basis.

People, philosophy, and process are all fuzzy concepts that are hard to measure and evaluate. As will be seen shortly, performance can also be misleading, because luck plays such a major role in short-term returns. But the cost of investing in a fund is straightforward, and it has a significant impact on return. Unfortunately, many people fail to focus on expenses, since they are withdrawn directly from the fund.

Price/Cost

Depending upon the kind of mutual fund that you choose, either one or two different types of fees will be levied against your capital. Annual expenses are charged against every fund, while sales charges apply only to "load" funds. Since annual expenses are fairly straightforward, these will be dealt with first.

The annual expense charge covers all of the basic costs of operating the fund, which include a fee paid to the fund's sponsor for providing investment advice, auditing fees, postage and printing costs, advertising, and so on. Every mutual fund prospectus includes a table with detailed information on expenses, and they are also covered in the mutual fund evaluation services. Generally, these expenses are expressed as a percentage of the value of the fund called the **expense ratio**. For example, the average domestic stock fund has a ratio of 1.4%, which means that the annual return on the fund will be reduced by that amount. International stock funds typically have a higher ratio of 1.7%, while bond funds are somewhat cheaper at 1%. You may recall the earlier discussion of index funds, which suggested that their superior return stems from their low cost. The largest S&P 500 Index Fund has an expense ratio of .2%, which means that it starts out with a 1.2% advantage over the average equity fund.

How can you compare the expense ratio of a fund with other alternatives? Services such as Morningstar regularly publish information on the average expense ratio for each category of funds. As indicated above, expense ratios vary according to the type of fund, making it important that you compare a given fund with the correct category. While a few funds have generated high enough returns to justify above-average fees, you should begin with the assumption that lower-cost funds are superior. Remember, capital markets are highly competitive, which makes it very difficult for any given fund to consistently outperform its peers. Therefore, a fund with a high expense ratio can be expected to deliver lower net returns than cheaper alternatives.

SALES CHARGES

Load funds are generally sold by stockbrokers, financial planners, and insurance agents, who receive a fee for their services called the **sales load**. Most sales loads are charged at the time of investment, and they reduce the amount of your money that is actually invested in the fund.

Here's how it works. An investor in a no-load fund buys in at the net asset value, which is calculated by dividing the total value of the fund by the number of shares outstanding. In other words, an investor who purchases a share in a no-load stock fund at a net asset value of $10 receives $10 worth of stocks. In contrast, the investor in a load fund pays the offering price, which is equal to the net asset value plus the sales charge. For example, she would pay $10.50 assuming a net asset value of $10 and a 5% sales charge. To put it bluntly, the load investor pays $10.50 to purchase $10 worth of stock. Historically, sales charges were as high as 8.5%. As a result of consumer resistance and competition, 5% or less is more common today.

Consumer resistance has also forced mutual fund sponsors to become more creative in the way that they levy sales charges. For example, some funds now charge a back-end load. In this case, no charge is assessed at the time of investment, but a fee is payable according to a declining scale if you decide to withdraw from the fund during the first five years.

Another popular option is the 12b-1 plan, in which an annual charge is added to the expense ratio to cover the up-front cost of marketing the fund. Finally, many funds now offer A, B, and C shares, which carry different combinations of up-front loads and annual charges. Sales loads must be disclosed in the fund's prospectus, and they are prominently displayed in the fund evaluation services as well. A very easy way to determine whether a fund charges a load is to check its listing in the mutual fund section of your newspaper. The price of a no-load fund will be shown as the net asset value. A load fund will be displayed with two different prices: the net asset value and the offering price.

Since thousands of no-load funds are available, under what circumstances does it make sense to purchase a load fund? First, you should be willing to pay the sales charge for a fund that clearly delivers a higher return than other alternatives after taking into account the load. However, both logic and empirical evidence suggest that load funds deliver lower net returns on average because of the drag imposed by the sales charge. Does that mean that all load funds represent poor investments? Of course not. Several load funds have delivered outstanding results. But should you count on those results in the future, and can you determine which other load funds are about to experience a change in fortune? The bottom line is that you should be very skeptical about paying a sales charge in order to get performance.

A second reason that is often used to justify a sales load is that you gain access to the expertise of the salesman. In fact, some salesmen are very knowledgeable about asset allocation, portfolio structuring, and retirement planning. They can be very helpful to an individual who is overwhelmed by the process of creating a retirement program. However, after reading this book you will know everything that is required to do a first-class job of managing your financial affairs. And, if you do feel the need for a little extra help, there are many low-cost sources of information that will be discussed in the next chapter.

We have now covered four of the five P's, which leaves only Performance. Ideally, performance or returns should be used only to confirm the impression of a fund that you developed by evaluating the other four factors. Unfortunately, most people fall into the trap of picking the fund with the best recent performance.

Performance

A very basic human tendency is to be highly influenced by recent experience. In the investment arena, this tendency translates into the belief that the best-performing investments will be those that have performed well recently. As you know, investors are inclined to invest in stocks after they have risen, because good returns give them a sense of comfort and safety. Similarly, mutual funds that perform well experience huge cash inflows as the media discovers a new financial guru and hopeful investors jump on board.

In reality, a number of studies of mutual fund performance have found that good returns over a five-year period have no predictive value for subsequent periods. To the extent that there is any relationship, these studies suggest that the better-performing funds in the first period are more likely to do poorly during the second. Why is this the case? As has been mentioned, luck is an important factor. Second, investment styles come into and out of favor. For example, when growth stocks are performing well, it comes as no surprise that a growth-oriented mutual fund outperforms the pack. When the cycle turns and value is in vogue, the growth fund is likely to be near the bottom. Finally, a successful fund is sure to attract more competition, which may take away any edge that it had. All of these factors suggest that short-term returns don't provide you with very much useful information. On the other hand, no rational person would invest in a fund without examining its track record. How, then, should returns be evaluated?

First, an apples-to-apples comparison requires that you examine returns net of all costs. Returns on mutual funds are reported after annual expenses but before any sales charges. Therefore, you must somehow incorporate sales charges in order to make the comparison meaningful. This analysis is somewhat arbitrary, because it requires that you spread the up-front charge over the number of years that you remain in the fund. Since you don't really know how long you will maintain your holding, a reasonable convention is to spread it over a period of about five years. For example, you would subtract 1% from the reported annual return on a fund that charges a 5% load. Second, don't forget that the track record is relevant only if the portfolio manager has been in place for a long time. Third, it is critical that a fund's performance be compared against other funds of the same type. Small capitalization stock funds should be compared with other aggressive stock funds, and so on. This comparison is relatively easy to make, because the fund evaluation services rank the past performance of a fund versus others in its category. In the same way, each fund should be compared against the relevant market index to ensure that the fund is adding value versus an index fund. The appropriate market index for each asset category was listed in the Index Fund section on page 141. Finally, longer track records are more meaningful. In fact, a period of twenty years is required to demonstrate that a manager has statistically outperformed a market index. Therefore, track records of five years or less are largely statistical noise.

Where do the mutual fund ratings of business magazines and fund evaluation services fit into all of this? Mutual fund evaluation services provide a great deal of information that should be of considerable assistance to you in the fund selection process. However, it is not clear that their performance ratings have much predictive value, which means that they should not represent the primary factor in your decision. Instead, a good use of these ratings is as a source of candidates. If your plan offers several highly ranked funds, they should certainly be included in the short list of funds that you carefully evaluate.

A PROCESS FOR SELECTING FUNDS

Now that you have considered the five P's, how do you actually go about selecting a fund? The process of picking a fund is analogous to a funnel in which a large number of candidates is narrowed down to a final selection. You should follow the same steps for both mutual funds and annuity products.

The first is to identify the funds that are available through your plan in each category. If only one option is provided, the decision is easy. In those categories in which more than one option is available, the next step is to go to your library and read up on the candidates using one of the evaluation services. You should focus on the tenure of the portfolio manager, the consistency of the fund's investment approach, cost, and performance. Of course, you are encouraged to rely on articles in the financial press, recommendations from industry experts, and any other information that is available to you.

At this point, you should tentatively select a finalist in each category. Then, ask for a prospectus on each finalist from the Human Resources department of your employer or by contacting the mutual fund sponsor directly (many have a toll-free number). While you may not enjoy slogging through the prospectus, it is particularly important that you read the "Investment Objectives and Guidelines" section to make sure that the fund's risk posture is consistent with your needs.

If you are comfortable with your tentative decision after reading the prospectus, then you are finally ready to actually implement your retirement plan. While this process is focused on picking one fund in each category, there is no harm in choosing several of them. In fact, the use of several funds will enhance both diversification and stability, though it will require a little more effort on your part.

ONGOING MONITORING

Once you have actually set up your retirement plan and are contributing to the funds that you have chosen, how do you monitor their performance over time? The process is identical to the one that you followed when evaluating the performance of initial candidates.

Most funds provide quarterly and annual reports that compare their results with those of similar funds and market indices. Shortly after the end of each quarter, the *Wall Street Journal* and other periodicals report returns for various categories of funds as well as for individual funds. In fact, year-to-date and twelve-month returns are reported daily in the *Wall Street Journal* for each fund. Finally, the fund evaluation services are regularly updated to reflect recent results. In addition to reviewing returns, you should periodically review the investment philosophy grids contained in the fund evaluation services to make sure that your fund has not changed its approach.

Just as it was dangerous to rely on recent results when selecting a fund, you should not pass judgment on your fund on the basis of short-term results. An individual who changes funds following a period of poor returns is almost certain to experience more of the same. The fund that was sold is likely to bounce back, while the new fund was undoubtedly chosen because of its great record—which means that it is primed for a fall. As long as the performance of your fund is in the ballpark of similar funds, don't worry about it.

When should you change funds? First, a change in portfolio managers provides a good reason to engage in a careful review of your fund. Second, any sign of a change in investment strategy represents grounds for divorce. Similarly, a major increase in the size of a fund should raise the caution flag, because an influx of assets is often followed by a change in approach. Finally, you should change funds after a sustained period of poor performance, lasting three to five years.

A PERSPECTIVE ON FUND SELECTION

While you should not take the process of selecting funds lightly, you also shouldn't lose any sleep over it. Remember, more than 90% of your return is a function of asset allocation, which means that the quality of your fund choices will have only a modest effect on the success of your retirement program. Moreover, the fact that your portfolio includes between four and six different funds reduces the potential impact of a poor choice in any single category.

As discussed in the next chapter, a large number of sources of information on mutual funds are readily available, and many are free of charge. By following the "funnel" approach to mutual fund selection, you will be able to use all of this information in an effective manner. While this approach is straightforward and manageable, index funds represent an even simpler solution that requires almost no effort on your part.

GRADUATION DAY

Congratulations! You now have covered all of the basic steps necessary to developing an organized retirement plan. In case you have any lingering doubts about your ability to implement your program, the final chapter includes some helpful information on resources that are available to support you along the way.

Key Points to Remember

- Index funds are likely to outperform most actively managed funds, and they represent the simplest means of constructing a diversified portfolio.

- If you want to invest in actively managed funds, make your selections based on a careful review of the "Five P's."

- Avoid selecting or changing funds on the basis of recent returns.

CHAPTER 8

Step Up to the Plate

You give 100 percent in the first half of the game, and if that isn't enough, you give what's left in the second half.

—Yogi Berra

A baseball motif was chosen for this last chapter because there are a number of similarities between investing and the national pastime. This analogy should tie together the variety of topics that have been covered.

A baseball team's manager develops a strategy for each game that includes the field assignments, the choice of pitcher, and the batting order. Likewise, the majority of this book has been devoted to creating a strategy for your retirement plan.

First, we settled on your primary objective, which was the standard of living that you hope to enjoy during retirement. This target dictated the amount of salary that you should be contributing to your retirement fund every year. We also considered the amount of risk that you are willing and able to assume. By using the best available technology, we converted capital market data into a portfolio structure that seems likely to deliver the highest possible return for the risk level that you selected. Finally, you learned how to select a team of mutual funds and insurance products to implement your retirement portfolio.

While each step is important, your success will depend largely on the quality of your overall strategy and not on the prowess of the portfolio managers that actually handle your money. As Yogi Berra also said, "You've got to be careful if you don't know where you are going because you might not get there."

Great baseball managers also have the ability to adjust their strategy as the game progresses. They know when to replace the pitcher or to substitute a pinch hitter. Sometimes, they intentionally walk a batter. Similarly, you now have the knowledge to monitor your retirement portfolio and to make any changes that are required. Once or twice a year, you will rebalance your portfolio back to the target weightings and conduct a brief review of the investment performance of each of your funds. As you approach the end of each phase in your financial life, you will also transition your portfolio to the next stage.

However, since most activity in the investment world is expensive and nonproductive, your interests will be best served by resisting the temptation to overmanage your portfolio. George Steinbrenner discovered that hiring and firing managers did not improve the fortunes of the New York

Yankees during the 1980s. For the same reason, switching mutual funds will not do much for your retirement program. Unless you are blessed with unusual insights, you should also avoid the urge to time markets.

Many of the characteristics of great baseball teams are also applicable to the investment management business. For example, winning teams play both good offense and good defense. The portfolios recommended in Chapter 6 included a healthy weighting in stocks, which provide the offense for your retirement program. At the same time, these portfolios are sufficiently diversified to ride out rough periods in the markets without causing too much pain.

Simply stated, diversification provides your defense. While home runs are nice, the most valued players are those with high batting averages. They hit lots of singles and doubles. Similarly, the team that wins the pennant is often the most consistent club, as opposed to the one with the most raw power. Both of these principles have guided the creation of your investment program. Because of their diversification, the four recommended portfolios will always underperform the "hot" investment of the day. But they will continue to plug along when last quarter's winner crashes and burns. To switch metaphors for a moment, retirement investing is a marathon and not a sprint.

Finally, a baseball team must take some risks in order to win it all. A bold strategy is occasionally required. Many retirement investors concentrate their assets in stable value and money market funds because they are unwilling to expose their money to the vagaries of the market. But unless they contribute extraordinary amounts to their retirement fund, timid investors will not enjoy the kind of retirement that they expect, because these vehicles do not deliver enough return to get the job done. You now have an understanding of the true nature of investment risk, which should provide you with the confidence to invest more aggressively.

A LITTLE HELP FROM MY FRIENDS

Casey Stengel said, "Managing a baseball team is a great job because you get paid for home runs that other people hit." In the same way, you can benefit from the large number of resources that are available to help you achieve your retirement goals.

As has been mentioned numerous times, the first place to go for help is the Benefits or Human Resources department of your employer. By law, companies that offer defined contribution plans are required to provide their employees with enough education to make informed decisions regarding their retirement options. Generally, they rely on educational materials that are prepared by the mutual fund vendors whose products are offered through the plan. Human Resources professionals are particularly knowledgeable about the administrative details of the plan as well as the government regulations that affect contributions, withdrawals, and so on. Your employer usually will stop short of giving you actual investment advice, but will ensure that you ask the right questions and consider all of the relevant factors.

FINANCIAL PLANNING SOFTWARE

If you are computer literate, a huge number of software packages are available to assist you in creating and maintaining your investment program. First, many of the mutual fund sponsors sell investment planning software. Just to name a few, Fidelity, T. Rowe Price, and Vanguard all offer very good programs for less than $20. They can be reached as follows:

Fidelity	800-544-9797
T. Rowe Price	800-541-1472
Vanguard	800-876-1840

These packages are easy to use, although each, not surprisingly, recommends its own funds. If you are interested in relatively objective advice, you may want to consider one of the more sophisticated packages that are produced by financial software vendors. One of the more popular option:

Quicken Financial Planner   800-446-8848

Most financial planning software packages follow more or less the same process of developing a plan that has been used in this book. However, they offer the added advantage of being able to incorporate other financial objectives, such as saving for college. Finally, some retirement fund vendors are willing to arrange a meeting with one of their representatives, who will use his organization's computer tools to help you develop a custom plan. Check with your Benefits department to see if this service is available.

MUTUAL FUND SELECTION

With the growth in the number of funds, a large industry has also developed to offer mutual fund information and advice. *Business Week, Forbes, Money,* and several other business publications have regular columns devoted to mutual funds as well as special "Mutual Fund" issues that appear several times a year. In Chapter 7, mutual fund evaluation services such as Morningstar were frequently referenced. Check with your local library to see if one of the following services is available:

CDA/Wiesenberger Mutual Funds Update
Morningstar Mutual Funds
Standard and Poors/Lipper Mutual Fund Profiles
Value Line

Several mutual fund services can also be purchased on either floppy disks or CD-ROM. These services, which are generally updated quarterly, allow you to screen for funds with certain characteristics. Two highly rated options are:

Morningstar Mutual Funds   800-876-5005
Mutual Fund Expert   800-237-8400

If you enjoy surfing the Internet, you might stop at a Web site called called Invest-O-Rama, which provides a link to more than 2,000 investment-related sites. Its address is

http://www.investorama.com

Finally, America Online, Compuserve, and Prodigy all provide a variety of on-line services related to investing.

FINANCIAL PLANNERS

If all of this technology leaves you longing for human contact, you always have the option of hiring a financial planner to assist you in developing your retirement program. Unless you have unusual or complex financial circumstances, you probably will be able to handle your own affairs successfully after reading this book, along with the materials furnished by your employer. But if you need further assistance, here are a few tips to help you find a planner who will meet your needs.

Some planners do not charge a fee for their services. Instead, they recommend investment products on which they are paid a sales charge or load. Since many people are unwilling to pay directly for financial advice, they are attracted to this structure. However, you should question whether the planner can be totally objective in his recommendations when his compensation is dependent on the vehicles that you choose. "Fee-only" planners do not sell products but charge directly for their services. While they probably provide more objective advice, you will be required to write a fairly significant check as payment for a comprehensive analysis.

Regardless of which type of planner you choose, you can take a few steps to check on his competency and integrity. First, you should call the Securities and Exchange Commission (800-732-0330) to find out if your planner is a registered investment advisor (RIA). While not required, this designation reduces the chance of fraud, because RIAs are subject to regulation and the SEC is equipped to handle consumer complaints regarding their professional behavior. Second, call the Certified Financial Planner Board of Standards at 303-830-7543, ext. 219, to find out whether a planner holds the Certified Financial Planner designation. CFPs are required to pass a comprehensive examination and must satisfy certain education and experience requirements. Additionally, they are bound by a professional code of ethics.

PLAY BALL!

This book has now covered everything you need to know about saving and investing. The patience, discipline, and commitment to follow through are up to you. You must demonstrate a commitment to saving and the discipline to continue saving when times are tough. Additionally, you must be committed to doing enough homework on the mutual funds that are available through your plan to make good choices. Most important, you will be required to be very patient when your investments decline in value during a market downturn. As is the case with most other forms of responsibility, these requirements are sometimes difficult and painful. But the potential payoff is tremendous, and you will be the beneficiary.

Step up to the plate!

Glossary

Annuity A contract in which an insurance company agrees to make income distributions for a specified period of time in return for one or more up-front payments. Many retirees choose an annuity as a safe way to receive their retirement benefits.

Appreciation An increase in the price or value of any asset. Over time, more than one-half of the return on stocks has come from appreciation.

Asset Any item of value. For example, stocks, bonds, and money market funds are financial assets, and they represent the most widely used asset classes.

Asset allocation The process of dividing your portfolio among different asset classes. The asset allocation decision largely determines the risk and return on your portfolio.

Balanced fund A mutual fund that invests in stocks, bonds, and money market securities. Balanced funds are designed for those who do not want to make their own asset mix decision.

Bond An IOU issued by a corporation or government. Bonds usually have a stated interest rate or coupon and a specific maturity date when the principal is to be repaid.

Capitalization The value of a company in the stock market. The capitalization is calculated by multiplying the price of the stock by the number of shares outstanding.

Common stock A share of the ownership of a corporation. The return on a common stock is determined by its dividend and any potential price appreciation. Also called *equity*.

Compound interest The process by which an investment earns not only interest, but interest on the interest that has been previously earned. The power of compounding allows an investor earning 9% to double her money in just eight years.

Correlation A statistical measure of the relationship between the returns on two different investments. Stable portfolios result from combining investments with low or negative correlation.

Currency risk Changes in the value of a non–U.S. investment as a result of fluctuations in the relationship between the U.S. dollar and other currencies.

Debt Any form of loan or obligation, including bonds, mortgages, or money market securities.

Default Failure by a borrower to make timely payments of interest or principal on a debt. This risk is particularly relevant to lower-quality, or "junk," bonds.

Defined benefit plan A pension plan in which the company promises to pay a retiree a benefit that is determined by a formula. In a DB plan, all of the funding and investment risk is retained by the company.

Defined contribution plan A retirement plan in which both the employee and employer make contributions and the employee shoulders all of the investment risk.

Diversification The process of spreading a portfolio among a number of different securities in order to reduce the impact of a decline in any single holding.

Dividend A payment to a stockholder, representing a portion of the company's profits. Dividends can be paid either in cash or in shares of stock.

Equity *See* Common stock.

Expense ratio The cost of operating a mutual fund, expressed as a percentage of the value of the fund. The annual expense ratio for the typical stock mutual fund is approximately 1.4%.

Index fund A mutual fund that attempts to equal the return on a specific market index by buying and holding all of the securities that make up that index. Index funds generally outperform at least 60% of actively managed funds.

Inflation Increases in the prices of goods and services. During this century, the average annual rate of inflation has been approximately 3%.

Lifestyle fund A diversified fund whose asset allocation is designed for individuals at a specific stage in life. These funds represent "one-stop shopping" for those who do not wish to manage their own investment program. Also known as a *life cycle fund*.

Liquidity A measure of how quickly and easily an investment can be sold. Highly liquid investments include government bonds and money market securities, while some smaller capitalization stocks are illiquid.

Load A sales charge that is levied at the time that a mutual fund is purchased. The load is the difference between the offering price and the net asset value.

Market timing An attempt to outperform a buy-and-hold strategy by timing the purchase and sale of different types of securities. Market timing is theoretically very profitable, but few practitioners have been successful in managing a timing program with real money.

Maturity The date on which the principal of a debt instrument is repaid.

Money market fund A mutual fund that invests in money market securities with an average maturity of approximately 60 days. Money market funds represent an attractive place to park temporary funds.

Mutual fund An investment fund in which a large number of individuals pool their money in order to be managed in a professional and efficient manner.

Net asset value The value of a mutual fund share, which is calculated by dividing the total value of the fund by the number of shares outstanding. The NAV is the price at which a no-load fund investor buys and sells shares.

Optimizer A computer program that determines the combination of different types of securities that delivers the highest expected return for a given level of risk. An optimizer provides helpful insights into portfolio construction but is only as good as its inputs.

Portfolio Any collection of securities. The risk of an individual investment is of importance only to the extent that it changes the risk of the overall portfolio.

Prospectus A legal document that must be provided to each person who invests in a mutual fund. The prospectus provides information regarding the fund's investment approach, expenses, and so on.

Rebalancing The process of returning portfolio weightings to target levels. Rebalancing is necessary because varying rates of return cause portfolio weightings to drift away from target levels.

Replacement ratio   An individual's desired level of retirement income, expressed as a percentage of his salary during the last year of employment. Most people should shoot for a replacement ratio of 80% to 90%.

Savings rate   The percentage of salary that should be contributed to a retirement fund in order to achieve the desired standard of living during retirement. The savings rate consists of both employee and employer contributions.

Stable value fund   A mutual fund that guarantees that each participant will be able to withdraw her money at a price equal to her initial investment plus interest. These funds are appropriate for those who cannot tolerate any volatility in the value of their investments.

Standard and Poors 500   An index of the 500 largest U.S. stocks. This index is often used as a proxy for the U.S. stock market and is the benchmark against which the performance of many funds is compared.

Standard deviation   A statistical measure of the amount by which the return on an investment fluctuates around its average return. An investment with a large standard deviation is risky, because its value at any given time is unpredictable. *See also* Volatility.

Tax deferral   An advantage enjoyed by retirement funds because no tax is payable on either contributions or growth until an individual begins receiving income during retirement.

Total return The sum of the dividend or interest on an investment and any change in price expressed as a percentage of the beginning value of the investment. During this century, the total return on stocks has averaged 10.5% per year.

Volatility Fluctuation in the price of an investment. *See* Standard deviation.

Yield The income on an investment, expressed as a percentage of its price. It is very important that yield not be confused with total return. A security with a high yield can suffer a negative return if the price drops by more than the income payment.

Index

Annuity
    definition of, 171
    designated period, 29
    fixed, 27–28, 64–65, 93
    joint-and-survivor, 29
    overview of, 27–28
    single life, 28, 30
    unit refund life, 29–30
    variable, 27–28
    as vehicle to accumulate retirement
        funds, 49
Appreciation
    definition of, 171
    as source for equity return, 50–52
Asset, definition of, 171
Asset allocation, 90, 94–96, 122–23, 129,
        130–32, 171
    and choosing portfolio, 122–23
    definition of, 171
    market timing, 130–32
    moving from one stage to next, 129
    power of, 95–96

Back-end load, 155
Balanced fund, 66, 67, 74, 171
    definition of, 171
    projected return of, 67
Bell-shaped curve for an investment,
        85–87
Bonds, 52–53, 58–62, 65–66, 67
    corporate, 59–60, 65
    definition of, 172
    foreign, 60, 66
    frequency of losses, 75
    historical returns on, 78, 79
    index funds and, 141
    issuer of, 59
    junk, 61, 66, 79
    long-term, 75

long-term government, 66, 74
maturity of, 60
money market mutual funds, 63
mortgage, 62
projected return of, 67
recommended mix of, 114
shortfall risk of, 88
short-term government, 61
U.S. government, 59
versus stocks, 59

Capitalization, definition of, 54, 172
"catch-up" provision for 403(b) plan, 15
Certified Financial Planner Board of
    Standards, 169
Chart 4.1: Power of diversification, 58
Chart 5.1: Relationship between risk and
    return, 72
Chart 5.2: Impact of time, 78
Chart 5.3: Bell-shaped curve, 85
Chart 5.4: Standard deviation, 86
Chart 5.5: Shortfall risk of stocks and
    bonds, 88
Chart 5.6: Power of diversification
    (Diverse portfolio), 92
Chart 6.1: Opitmal portfolios, 108
Chart 6.2: Recommended portfolios'
    risk/return tradeoff, 117
College tuition, borrowing from
    retirement plans for payment of, 18
Common stock, definition of, 172
Compound interest, 3–4, 172
    definition of, 172
Contributions to retirement plan, 15–16,
    33–46, 125–28
    allocating, 125–28
    how much, 33–46
Corporate bonds, 59–60, 65
Correlation, definition of, 172

Currency fluctuations and international stock and bond funds, 152
Currency risk, definition of, 172
Current income, as source for equity return, 50

DB plan. *See* Defined benefit plan
DC plan. *See* Defined contribution plan
Debt
 definition of, 172
 instruments, 52–53
Default, definition of, 173
Defined benefit plan, 12–14
 definition of, 173
 versus defined contribution plan, 12–14
Defined contribution plan, 12–14
 basic structure of, 13, 21
 definition of, 173
 employee benefits, 13
 versus defined benefit plan, 12–14
Department of Labor, 11
Dependent, joint-and-survivor annuity and, 29
Designated period annuity, 29
Diverse portfolio, 92–93
Diversification, 57–58, 90–94, 163, 173
 definition of, 173
 power of, 57–58
Dividend, definition of, 173
Double bet on a company, 68

EAFE (Europe, Australia, Far East Index), 142
Early accumulation stage, 97–98, 117
 recommended portfolio for, 117
Emotional makeup and risk, 102
Employee, benefit of defined contribution plan, 13
Employers
 changing, transferring retirement plan funds, 18–19
 retirement plans for types of, 14
 retirement plans, warning about, 68
Equity, 49–50, 173
 definition of, 173
 sources of return, 50

Expense ratio, 142, 150, 154, 173
 definition of, 173
 and 12b-1 plan, 156

Fee-only planners, 169
Finance, cardinal rule of, 123–24
Financial planners, 168–69
Financial planning software, 166–67
Financial responsibilities, and risk, 101
Fixed annuity, 27–28, 64–65, 93
Foreign bond funds, 60, 66, 152
 and currency fluctuation philosophy, 152
Foreign stock, 54, 56–57, 67, 74, 114, 141–43, 152
 and currency fluctuation philosophy of fund, 152
 frequency of losses, 74
 index funds and, 141–43
 projected return of, 67
 recommended mix of, 114
For-profit company, retirement plan for, 14
401(k) plan, 2, 3, 7, 13, 14, 15
 employee contribution for, 15–16
 hardship provision of, 17–18
 investment categories in, 47
403(b) plan, 3, 13, 14
 "catch-up" provision for, 15
 employee contribution for, 15–16
 hardship provision of, 17–18
 investment categories in, 47
457 plan, 3, 13, 14
 employee contribution for, 15
 hardship provision of, 18
 transferring if you change employers, 19
Fund size of mutual funds, 150–51
Funnel approach to mutual fund selection, 162

Glossary, 171–77
Growth philosophy of equity investment, 147–48
Guaranteed fund, 64

Index • 181

Hardship provision of retirement plans, 17–18
Household formation stage, 97, 117
 recommended portfolio for, 117
Human capital, 101
Human Resources department, 8, 11

Index funds, 138–43, 173
 definition of, 173
 pros and cons of, 140–41
 setting up retirement portfolio with, 141–43
Individual retirement account. *See* IRA
Inflation
 definition of, 174
 protection for single life annuity, 30
Intelligent Investor, The, 135
Intermediate-term bonds, 61
Internal Revenue Service, 11, 20–21
 requirement for retirement plan benefit payments, 20–21
Investment
 bell-shaped curve for, 85–87
 major category of, 52
 options, 110–11
 primer on, 47–69
  annuity, 49
  mutual fund, 48–49
 program, five steps to an, 6
 projected return of popular options, 67
 risk, 71–103
 risk versus return, 58
IRA
 Rollover account
  evaluating firms for, 24–25
  transferring retirement funds to, 19
 SEP-, 14, 15
Issuer of bonds, 59

Joint-and-survivor annuity, 29
Junk bonds, 61, 66, 79, 149

Large capitalization stocks, 54–55, 67
 frequency of losses, 74
 frequency of significant losses, 75–76
 index funds and, 141–43

projected return of, 67
recommended mix of, 114
Lehman Government/Corporate Index, 142
Life cycle
 early accumulation stage, 97–98
 household formation stage, 97
 maximum accumulation stage, 97–98
 retirement state, 97, 98–99
Life cycle approach
 moving from one stage to next, 129
 to risk, 96–100
Lifestyle fund, 124, 174
 definition of, 174
 mutual funds, 124
Liquidity, definition of, 174
Load, definition of, 174
Load funds, 154, 156
Loan provisions in retirement plans, 17
Long-term bonds, 60–61, 75
 frequency of significant losses, 75
Long-term government bond, 66, 74
 frequency of losses, 74
Losses, temporary versus permanent, 79–80
Lump sum distribution of retirement plan benefits, 25

Management of funds, active versus passive, 138
Market timing
 definition of, 174
 perils of, 130–32
Maturity
 of bonds, 60
 definition of, 174
Maximum accumulation stage, 97–98, 117
 recommended portfolio for, 117
Medicare, 2
Middle-of-the-road portfolios, 114
Money market funds, 52, 53–64, 67, 74, 114, 174
 definition of, 174
 mutual funds, 63–64, 67
 projected return of, 67
 recommended mix of, 114
Morningstar, 146, 149, 154

Mortgage bond funds, 62
Mutual fund, 7, 48–49
　balanced funds, 66
　definition of, 175
　foreign stocks, 57
　index funds, 138–43
　lifestyle, 124
　matching to asset classes, 136–37
　money market, 63–64
　ongoing monitoring of, 160–61
　overview of selecting, 143–59
　　people, 143, 144–46
　　performance, 157–59
　　philosophy, 146–52
　　price, 153–59
　　process, 153
　selecting, 6, 135, 159–60, 161–62, 167–68
　　perspective on, 161–62
　　process for, 159–60
　stock, 55, 57, 93
　　diversification of, 93
　U.S. government bond, 59

Net asset value, definition of, 175
No-load fund, 156
Not-for-profit entity, retirement plan for, 14

Optimization programs, 109, 110–13, 122–23
　and choosing portfolio, 122–23
Optimizer, definition of, 175
Options of retirement income, key considerations in selecting, 22–24

Partial or periodic withdrawal of plan benefits upon retirement, 26
People/organization involved in managing mutual funds, 144–46
Percentage of income to contribute to retirement, 41–44
Performance of mutual fund investments, 157–59
Permanent loss, examples of, 79–80

Philosophy of mutual fund investment, 146–52
　bond, 149–50
　currency, 152
　equity, 147
　fund size, 150–51
　funky securities, 151
Portable funds, 13–14
Portfolio
　allocating your contributions, 125–28
　asset mix, 94–96
　concept of, 106–7
　creating a, 105–33
　definition of, 175
　Diverse, 92–93
　growth- versus value-oriented stock fund, 148
　incorporating company stock into asset allocation, 120–21
　investment options, 110–11
　and life cycle, 116–17
　market timing, 130–32
　measures of risk, 119
　moving from one stage to next, 129
　optimal, 107–8
　projected annual returns of, 118
　rebalancing, 125–28
　recommended, 113–16
　and risk, 108–13
　　investment options, 110–11
　　optimization programs, 109, 110–13
　　risk and return forecasts, 111
Price/cost of mutual funds, 153–59
　sales charges, 155–57
Process of investment manager, 153
Prospectus, definition of, 175

Rebalancing
　definition of, 175
　portfolio, 125–28
Replacement ratio, 37–38, 40, 41–42, 172
　definition of, 176
　determining a savings rate, 41–42
　integrating Social Security, 40, 41–44
Residence, purchase of, 18
Resources, and risk, 101

Retirement, income during
  evaluating, 36–38
  strategies for saving, 44–45
Retirement, preparing for
  three rules for, 5
  getting organized, 6–8
  saving consistently, 5–6
  sticking with the program, 8
Retirement plan, 2, 3
  ABCs of, 11–31
  contributions to, 15–16
  employer's, double bet, 68
  how much to contribute to, 33–46
  income upon retirement
    lump sum distribution of, 25
    partial withdrawal of, 26
    options for, consideration in selecting, 22–24
  loan provisions in, 17
  moving funds from one investment option to another, 19–20
  ongoing monitoring of, 160–61
  portfolio, investments in, 6
  projected returns of popular options, 67
  rebalancing, 128
  setting up an indexed portfolio, 141–43
  taking money out of, 16–18
  transferring if you change employers, 18–19
  when you are required to withdraw funds from, 20–21
Retirement stage, 97, 98–99
  recommended portfolio for, 117
Return
  of portfolios, projected annual, 118
  and risk forecasts, 111
  versus risk, 67, 72, 85–87
    bell-shaped curve for investment, 85–87
Reviewing investment program, 6, 7
RIA (registered investment advisor), 169
Risk
  of coming up short of meeting retirement income objectives, 87
  controlling, 7, 90, 94–96
  asset allocation, 90, 94–96
  diversification, 90–94
  importance of, 72–73
  of investment, 71–103
    life cycle approach to, 96–100
    of losing money, 73–78
    and market timing, 130–32
    personalizing, 100–102
      emotional makeup and risk, 102
      financial responsibilities, and risk, 101
      human capital, 101
      resources, and risk, 101
      time, impact on risk, 100
    in perspective, 89–90
    and return forecasts, 111
    versus return, 67, 72, 85–87
      bell-shaped curve for investment, 85–87
    volatility, 81–87
Rollover account, transferring retirement funds to, 19
Russell 2000 Index, 142

Sales load, 155–56
S&P 500 Index. *See* Standard and Poors 500 Index
SAR-SEP, 14
Savings rate, definition of, 176
Securities and Exchange Commission, 48, 169
Self-employed individuals, retirement plans for, 14
SEP, 13, 14
SEP-IRA, 14, 15
  employee contribution for, 15
Short-term bonds, 60–61, 63
SIMPLE plan, 14
Single life annuity, 28, 30
  with inflation protection, 30
Small capitalization stocks, 54, 55–56, 67, 74, 75–76, 114, 141–43
  frequency of losses, 74
  frequency of significant losses, 75–76
  index funds and, 141–43
  projected return of, 67
  recommended mix of, 114

Social Security, 2, 38, 41–44
  integrating into retirement income, 38, 41–44
Software, financial planning, 166–67
Stable value fund, 64–65, 67, 74, 79, 81, 88–89, 93, 114, 176
  definition of, 176
  red flag for, 64–65
  projected return of, 67
  recommended mix of, 114
Standard and Poors 500 Index, 50, 55, 58, 138, 139, 176
  definition of, 176
Standard deviation
  definition of, 176
  of return, 86
Standard of living, during retirement, determining, 6–7
Stocks, 49–52, 54–58, 59, 74, 75, 76–78, 88, 93
  foreign, 54, 56–57, 74
  historical returns on, 76–78
  large capitalization, 54–55, 67, 74, 75
  mutual funds, 93
  shortfall risk of, 88
  small capitalization, 54, 55–56, 67, 74, 75
  versus bonds, 59
Surviving spouse
  effect of single life annuity on, 29
  joint-and-survivor annuity and, 29
Systematic withdrawal of retirement plan benefits, 26

Table 3.1: Determining a savings rate, 41–42
Table 3.2: Asset adjustment factor, 43–44
Table 4.1: Bond price sensitivity, 61
Table 4.2: Popular retirement plan options ranked by risk/return, 67
Table 5.1: Frequency of losses (1926–1996), 74
Table 5.2: Frequency of significant losses (1926–1996), 75
Table 5.3: Historic returns on stocks (1901–1996), 76
Table 5.4: Asset allocation decision (1901–1996), 95
Table 5.5: Life cycle approach to risk, 97
Table 6.1: Recommended asset mixes, 114
Table 6.2: Structure of 1,500 largest tax-exempt funds, 115
Table 6.3: Recommended portfolios for life cycles, 117
Table 6.4: Projected annual returns of portfolios, 118
Table 6.5: Measures of risk, 119
Table 6.6: Company stock in portfolio, 121
Target weightings, 128
Tax deferral
  benefits of, 34–36
  definition of, 176
Temporary loss, 79
Time
  impact on risk, 100
  as major influence on investment, 78–79
Torpedo stocks, 148
Total return, definition of, 177
Treasury bills, 63
12b-1 plan, 156

Unit refund life annuity, 29–30
U.S. Treasury bond, 52–53

Value approach to equity investment, 148–49
Value Line, 146
Variable annuity, 27–28
Vesting date, 13
Volatility
  definition of, 177
  of return, 81–87
  understanding, 84–87

Withdrawal of accumulated funds in retirement plan, 13

Yield, definition of, 177